2021 GAME ON!

THE ULTIMATE GUIDE TO GAMING!

2021 GAME ON!

Editor: Stuart Andrews

Design and Repro:
Andrew Sumner

Proofreader: Rachel Storry

Contributors:
Barry Collins, Robert Leane

ISBN 978-1-338-67087-5
10 9 8 7 6 5 4 3 2 1
20 21 22 23 24
Printed in the U.S.A. 40
First printing, November 2020

OVERWATCH 2
Blizzard's blockbuster FPS is back with reworked heroes and a brand-new co-op campaign. Is it good enough to beat Apex Legends and Valorant? Turn to pg.56 to find out!

STAY SAFE, HAVE FUN

■ Games are brilliant, but you need to know how to stay safe while you're playing, especially when you're playing online. Follow these simple rules to have a great time, then your parents won't need to worry about what you're playing or who you're playing with.

1 Talk to your parents and agree some rules on which games you can play online, when you can play them, how you'll talk to other players, and which websites and apps you can use.

2 Never give out any personal information while you're gaming, including your real name, where you live, your parents' names, where you go to school, any passwords, or your phone number.

3 Never agree to meet someone you've met online or through a game in person.

4 Tell your parents or a teacher if you find something online that makes you feel uncomfortable or scared.

5 Be nice to other people and players, even when you're competing against them. Don't say anything that might hurt someone's feelings or make them feel sad.

6 Take regular breaks when you're gaming. Give your eyes, hands, and brain a rest, and get your body moving.

7 Don't download or install any games or software without first checking with your parents and whoever owns the console, smartphone, tablet, or computer.

8 Pay attention to age ratings on games. They exist to protect you from content that might upset or disturb you, or that your parents won't be comfortable with you experiencing. They're not there as some kind of skill rating!

9 If you play mobile games outside, keep aware of your surroundings. Don't play them alone and wander around the neighborhood. Have a friend or family member with you.

10 If you use streaming services, check with a parent or adult before switching to a different video or game.

CONTENTS

30

70

40

50

84

126

208

108

28

32

120

98

GET YOUR GAME ON!

72 Sea of Thieves

40 Super Consoles

34 Minecraft Dungeons

22 Pokémon Sword and Shield

MINECRAFT DUNGEONS

178 Animal Crossing: New Horizons

112 Valorant

56 Overwatch 2

90 Fortnite

I t's been a historic year for all kinds of reasons, but gaming has given us comfort, fun, and some much-needed distraction along the way. We've looked back into the glorious past with reboots and remakes, including a fantastic start to the reworked Final Fantasy VII. We've looked forward into the future with games as exciting as Overwatch 2 and Dreams.

We've seen beloved series deliver their best games yet, with Luigi's Mansion 3 and Pokémon Sword and Shield, and the greatest online games go from strength to strength, with Roblox, Fortnite, Apex Legends, and Sea of Thieves.

And what makes this year even more amazing is that we're at the start of a new console generation, with the Xbox Series X and PS5 almost ready to roll out. We're set to have even more spectacular games in the years ahead, but there's still plenty of life in the games machines we have right now!

50 GREATEST GAMING MOMENTS

All the highlights from one amazing year

RETURN OF THE JEDI
STAR WARS JEDI: FALLEN ORDER

■ Just when it felt like we'd never see another great Star Wars game, along comes Respawn—the maker of Apex Legends—with something incredible. Fallen Order nailed both the Star Wars feel and the gameplay, borrowing from games as different as Dark Souls and Uncharted, then throwing in all the lightsaber duels, stormtrooper battles, and mystic moments you could want. The Force is strong in this one.

CALL IT A COMEBACK
APEX LEGENDS

■ We loved Apex Legends when it first came out. Then we got bored of the battles and tired of the tedious Battle Pass, then drifted back to Fortnite and the other battle royale games. Another team might have given up, but Apex came back fighting. Each season has brought in new maps, weapons, and game heroes to keep the action fresh. Sorry, Fortnite—Apex isn't going anywhere.

BUSTING GHOSTS
LUIGI'S MANSION 3

■ Hasn't Luigi always been the coolest Mario brother? Sure, he's a yellow-bellied coward who can't go through a door without trembling, but floor after floor he plucks up his courage, steadies his nerve, and starts sucking up the hotel's vengeful ghosts. Packing in more crazy hotel floors than you'd find in Vegas, Luigi's Mansion 3 puts the guy in green on top.

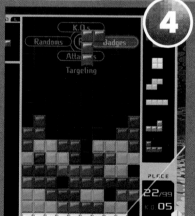

THE REAL BATTLE ROYALE
TETRIS 99

■ Think Fortnite is the ultimate battle royale, or that Apex Legends takes the crown? Those in the know understand that there's one more contender, and it's the nerve-shredding Tetris 99. Nintendo's Switch exclusive has up to 99 players fighting in one block-sorting battle, and nothing beats the feeling when you finish a line and know another player is going to get trashed.

5

HULK SMASH
MARVEL'S THE AVENGERS
■ This epic Avengers blockbuster couldn't deliver the stars of the movies, but it gets one incredible Hulk. Hulk smashes. Hulk trashes. Hulk jumps down and leaves a big dent in the ground. He slaps away puny soldiers like so many gnats, and grabs a handful of truck as he wall-runs over gaps. Other games have struggled to capture the sheer awesome power of Marvel's green giant. This one smashes it out of the park.

7

HORNET STINGS
HOLLOW KNIGHT: SILKSONG
■ Few games create a world as rich and strange as the insect fantasy kingdoms of Hollow Knight, so it's great to see Team Cherry repeat the trick with the stunning sequel, SilkSong. Hornet always felt too big to play a supporting role in somebody else's game. SilkSong makes her the star—and she owns the screen.

6

HONK, HONK!
UNTITLED GOOSE GAME
■ Who'd have thought that one of last year's most-loved games would be a left field indie hit about a small English village and one very naughty goose? There's nothing nice about harassing shopkeepers and gardeners or scaring a kid until he hides in a phone booth, but when you're a large and aggressive farm bird, it all seems perfectly all right. Brilliantly bad behavior.

8

THE WHOLE
SAIYAN SAGA
DRAGON BALL Z:
KAKAROT
■ While almost every animé adaptation works hard to treat the fans, Dragon Ball Z: Kakarot leaves no stone unturned in re-creating the whole darn Dragon Ball Z saga. It's not just about the battles, but about all the stuff that goes on in between, bringing in many of the silly, bizarre side stories that have kept fans puzzled for years. This is what you call fan service.

FIRE ON THE DECKS
SEA OF THIEVES

■ Sea of Thieves keeps getting better, with more treasures and secrets to discover as you sail its high seas. It's also a game where things can go wrong, where chaos rules, and a disaster is only a slip away. Adding firebombs created a whole new layer of craziness, as flames sweep the decks and you race for the nearest bucket. Sadly, it's not always the enemy to blame.

GOTTA CATCH 'EM ALL, ONLINE
TEMTEM

■ Pokémon felt like it was begging for the World of WarCraft treatment, so a small independent team used it as inspiration for a monster-collecting massive multiplayer game. Exploring, building your team of creatures, and training them never gets tired, but when you can do it with other players, it just gets better—especially when you battle them online.

GAMING'S GOT TALENT
NINJA GOES TO MIXER

■ The world of streaming now has its own stars, and they're bigger than the platforms that stream them. When Ninja moved to Mixer, his fans feared the worst, but since the move he's been playing better and enjoying himself more on stream. Other star streamers are signing their own deals, and if it means they're getting the money they deserve without getting exhausted, we're all for it.

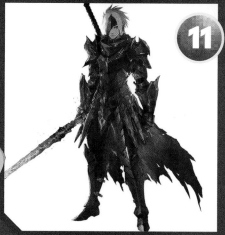

TWO WORLDS COLLIDE
TALES OF ARISE

■ Bandai Namco's Tales series never gets the credit it deserves, but with Tales of Arise there's no excuse: it's a must-have RPG. Its tale of two clashing worlds is epic, but it has strong characters and plenty of heart. It's got scenery worthy of a Final Fantasy, and a cool combat system that goes heavy on the action. Tales, your moment has arrived.

13

A WHOLE NEW WORLD
JOURNEY TO THE
SAVAGE PLANET

■ Explore strange new worlds, scan extraterrestrial life-forms, and turn weird vegetation and alien rubbish into tools and weapons to help you survive. Heaps of games do this kind of stuff. But what they don't have is such incredible sci-fi landscapes, so much goo, or so many odd little critters with noisy guts.

DUELLING
WIZARDS
SPELLBREAK

14

■ We love a good death match or Battle Royale, but where's the magic? In Spellbreak, it's right there on the screen. Here, teams of sorcerers battle it out with spells and enchantments—and Harry Potter never did it quite like this. Fly, throw fireballs, freeze the ground, and slide along it. If you've got the magic mastery of Doctor Strange, you can fight and win.

15

MOBILE GAMES ON TAP
APPLE ARCADE

■ Just when you think you're getting tired of mobile gaming—all the endless clones and dodgy pay-to-win games—along comes Apple and shakes up the whole thing. As a subscription service, Apple Arcade dishes up new games every week, and the developers are free to make smarter games that aren't always hustling you for money. It makes having an iPhone or iPad worth your while.

22 MINUTES TO SAVE
THE SOLAR SYSTEM
THE OUTER WILDS

16

■ You're an astronaut resting on a distant planet. In 22 minutes, the sun will go supernova, destroying all life, including yours. What can you discover in that time to stop the catastrophe, and what can you do to change your fate? A fantastic game sliced into repeated 22-minute playthroughs, where there's almost too much to explore. Amazing.

17

LEGENDS GO MOBILE
LEAGUE OF LEGENDS WILD RIFT

■ We've seen our share of mobile MOBAs, but none have really felt like the real deal. That changes with League of Legends Wild Rift, which downsizes one of the world's biggest online games in order to make it work on a smaller screen. You lose some of the scale but none of the strategy, and you still get to play with a huge roster of legendary heroes and villains.

SURVIVE THE BACKYARD
GROUNDED

18

■ Nothing puts things in perspective like being shrunk to the size of a bug, and Grounded makes it all feel real. You might think your back yard isn't dangerous, but puddles, angry beetles, and giant-sized ants aren't the only perils you face. Get together with friends, craft some armor, and build yourself a fort—and you might just live to see another sunrise.

19

20

KEEP THE GAMES COMING
XBOX GAMES PASS

■ When it first launched, Xbox Games Pass seemed crazy. Pay $9.99 a month and you got to play a growing library of games—and Microsoft even threw its top exclusive Xbox games on top. Since then, Games Pass has just gotten better, throwing in some of the biggest games from the biggest studios and the hottest indie games as well. It makes every month feel like Christmas!

DANCE THROUGH THE DUNGEONS
CADENCE OF HYRULE

■ For years, Link has messed around with Master Swords, hookshots, bows, and magic potions, when all he needed to save Hyrule was a decent beat and some dancing shoes (or maybe boots). Cadence of Hyrule mixes the rhythm action of Crypt of the Necrodancer with the world of Legend of Zelda, creating an action RPG where the music matters. Switch it on and do your best not to groove along.

SPONGEBOB'S BACK
SPONGEBOB SQUAREPANTS: BATTLE FOR BIKINI BOTTOM, REHYDRATED

■ The original Battle for Bikini Bottom didn't look bad for a PS2 game, but did it really do justice to SpongeBob, Squidward, and their world? Not really. This "rehydrated" remaster, however, makes the game look as good as a Pixar movie, without losing any of that classic SpongeBob style. Most of all, it makes us laugh.

21

CAT-CRAZY ANTICS
MINEKO'S NIGHT MARKET

■ So what if it looks like a version of Animal Crossing built by someone who really loves cats? It has cat racing, feline sumo wrestling, and what looks an awful lot like octopus tug-of-war. It's got more feline friends than the craziest cat lady and an island full of mysteries to solve. Throw away your doubts—this is a meow-velous game.

22

23

GOING UNDERGROUND
MINECRAFT DUNGEONS

■ Not every big game series can jump from one style of game to another, but Minecraft managed it with Minecraft Dungeons. Mojang delivered a fast-paced action RPG that feels like a less bloodthirsty Diablo, that's fun just to pick up and play with friends but also has a bit of staying power. It's the sort of game you play for just half an hour after dinner then, whoops, it's bedtime!

THE ASHEN WOLVES
FIRE EMBLEM: THREE HOUSES

■ With Fire Emblem: Three Houses, Nintendo already had one of the best tactical RPGs. The Cindered House DLC only gave us more to love. Now, as well as fighting battles and organizing tea with your favorite students, you have a new secret house and hidden underworld area to explore. The cool, rebellious Ashen Wolves might just become your new teacher's pets.

24

BECOMING IRON MAN
MARVEL'S IRON MAN VR

25

■ You'll never play a game that makes you feel like Iron Man, right? Wrong. With PSVR behind it, Marvel's Iron Man VR puts you right in those big metal boots. You can fly, blast your repulsor rays, save falling jets, and battle a mysterious new foe. It might not have Robert Downey Jr., but this is the best Iron Man experience on a console.

WE ARE THE CHAMPIONS!
FORTNITE WORLD CUP

26

■ Fortnite's not the first or the greatest eSport, but it's the one that's grabbing all the headlines. What's so great about it is that, for all the star players and multimillion-dollar prize money, it's still a game where ordinary kids can start playing, build their skills, and compete, and have a shot at a place in the finals. When teams and franchises aren't all-important, anyone has a shot at the title.

FORTNITE WORLD CUP

CLASSIC GAMES REMASTERED
AGE OF EMPIRES II AND WARCRAFT III

27

■ Your mom or dad might remember a golden age of PC gaming, where smart, exciting strategy games took you to the biggest battles in history or the wars that forged a fantasy kingdom. Well, those games are back, looking better than ever, and they still have a power and depth that some more recent games have lost, if you want to give them a shot.

MINECRAFT MEETS LIFE
MINECRAFT EARTH

28

■ We used to think augmented reality was a gimmick, but then came Pokémon GO. Now Minecraft has gone one step further, making it possible to build up from your kitchen table or dig down through your lawn. You can build a house, hunt for treasure, or get together with friends and have a skeleton-battling adventure. With Minecraft Earth, you can bring your wildest Minecraft fantasies out into the real world.

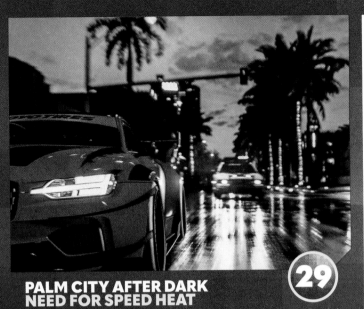

NEW CHALLENGERS
SUPER SMASH BROS.
ULTIMATE

30

■ The Switch Super Smash Bros. is the gift that keeps on giving. You can spend days unlocking all its heroes, but Nintendo keeps releasing even more! Joker, Banjo, and Byleth were reason enough to invest in the first fighters pass, and now we wait anxiously to find out which gaming superstars Nintendo is going to add next. Bring'em on!

PALM CITY AFTER DARK
NEED FOR SPEED HEAT

29

■ Need for Speed Heat is the best Need for Speed in years. That's partly because it has the best setting. By day, Palm City is a Florida beach paradise, primed for racing if you can just avoid the corrupt cops. By night, though, it's a neon wonderland, where illegal street races take you somewhere fast, furious, and thrilling. Hit the streets, rev the engine, and drive.

31

DREAMS (FINALLY) COME TRUE

■ Dreams has been a long time coming, but we're finally seeing all those amazing ideas realized, not just as a platform to make games but as a game in its own right. It's a game that asks you to use your imagination and create something special, but it shows you how to do it first. Whether you want to create great games or just explore them, it's a magical adventure.

PEDAL POWER
LONELY MOUNTAINS:
DOWNHILL

32

■ Games don't have to be complex. Sometimes all it takes is a simple idea. How about a game where you ride a mountain bike through tricky downhill courses, praying that your tires hold on to the loose gravel track just long enough to sweep around the next corner? Lonely Mountains: Downhill captures the excitement of mountain biking—and anyone can pick it up and play.

NOW EVERYONE'S A LEGEND
DESTINY 2

33

■ After Fortnite, Warframe, and Dauntless, online games are finding new ways to make money. It's no longer about paid-for games or monthly subscriptions, but about getting as many players online as possible, then selling them cosmetics, upgrades, and expansions. When it works, you don't have to pay to play or win, which means everyone gets a chance to sample games as epic as Bungie's classic. We're not going to complain about that.

WATCHING THE ORANGUTANS
PLANET ZOO

34

■ Planet Zoo is a dream for fans of the Discovery Channel, with its gorgeous gorillas, entertaining elephants, and lovable lions and tigers. But if you're looking for an animal that's great for guests and fun to watch, the Borneo Orangutan wins every time. You could watch these guys climb, eat, and groom themselves for hours—and you might even learn a thing or two!

36

DEER DIARY
WAY TO THE WOODS

35

■ In 2015, a lone teenage developer started sharing images of Way to the Woods: a game about two deer in a post-apocalyptic landscape with haunting visuals influenced by Studio Ghibli animations. Five years later, we can finally play it, and it's as strange and magical as we had hoped. It's an amazing achievement for the 19-year-old Anthony Tan, and a game you've just got to play.

MINDBOGGLING
PSYCHONAUTS 2

■ Lots of games like to make out that they're weird and crazy, but Psychonauts 2 looks and feels the part. Raz's world of mind-invading superspies is one where nothing makes sense but anything can happen, and where you'll be diving deep inside the shattered brains of the world's worst oddballs, eccentrics, and paranoid dentists. Sweet and surreal.

17

37

ZERO HOUR
OVERWATCH 2

■ We always loved the characters and worked away at their backstories, but from the initial announcement trailer Overwatch 2 has brought us closer to our heroes and explored the Overwatch lore. What's more, the co-op campaign gives us a whole new way to enjoy this fantastic FPS. If you thought you could walk out on the watch, think again.

GREAT ESCAPES
ORI AND THE WILL
OF THE WISPS

38

■ Moon Studios has given us what might be the most beautiful 2D platform game ever, then packed it with screen-filling monstrosities guaranteed to give you nightmares. Luckily, Ori is one of gaming's fastest and most acrobatic heroes, which comes in handy when you're being chased by giant spiders, creepy bugs, and angry beasts. Can your nerves take the pressure?

SEPIROTH
REBORN
FINAL FANTASY
VII REMAKE

40

■ Final Fantasy VII isn't short of brilliant characters and much-loved moments. There's a reason why Cloud, Aerith, Tifa, and Barret have become gaming legends. Yet nothing beats those heart-stopping moments where Sepiroth enters the tale. This is one of gaming's greatest and most mysterious villains, and he's never looked more absolutely awesome.

ISLAND LIFE
ANIMAL CROSSING: NEW HORIZONS

39

■ Life is hard. You've got school, homework, and chores to get through. Would it hurt to have a bit of time to chill? Then along comes a new Animal Crossing and you're in your own island paradise, shooting the breeze with Flip and Rosie, fishing, picking fruit, and doing all the usual crazy stuff—even making your own furniture. Now, that's the life!

JUMPING INTO CHAPTER 2 FORTNITE

41

■ The opening of Fortnite Chapter 2 was sheer showmanship at work. We had the wait, then the intro video, then that moment where you watched a player jump out of the bus, and realized you were now in control. Since then, we've had a new map, new vehicles, new weapons, new movie tie-ins, and a whole lot more, and it's every bit as unmissable as the best bits of Chapter 1.

42

Project xCloud
[P R E V I E W]
Play 50+ Xbox games on your mobile phone or tablet

43

DRAWN TO LIFE SABLE

■ Adventure games with cool cartoon graphics aren't anything new, but there's more to Sable than its cel-shaded style, which mimics the look of classic French comic books. It's the story of a young girl exploring a strange desert landscape, searching for signs of its secret history, and it's full of moments of magic and wonder that you just can't wait to share.

GAMES MEET CLOUD
GOOGLE STADIA AND MICROSOFT XCLOUD

■ Console gaming isn't going anywhere, but the new cloud gaming services make it possible to play in a whole new way. Play on your TV, your laptop, your tablet, or your phone. Play anywhere you can get a decent Internet connection. And, believe us, nothing beats playing games as big as Destiny 2 or Halo on your phone, especially when you can start where you left off on the big TV screen.

GO LITE!
NINTENDO SWITCH LITE

44

■ Not everyone needs a console they can plug into their TV, and with the Switch Lite, Nintendo fans now have a choice. If, like us, you do most of your Switch gaming outside of the lounge, you now have something smaller, lighter, less expensive, and a little bit tougher, and it still plays all the Switch's greatest games. We love the colors, too.

THE ULTIMATE STAR WARS BLOCKBUSTER LEGO STAR WARS: THE SKYWALKER SAGA

■ Think all nine Star Wars episodes would be too much for one game? Think again. The Skywalker Saga has all the action from all the movies, with all the heroes from Qui-Gon Jinn to Rey and all the villains from Darth Maul to Kylo Ren. More amazingly, it hits all the right notes of action, adventure, and comedy. If this doesn't make you whoop with joy, you don't love Star Wars.

45

48

YOUR NEXT ODYSSEY GODS & MONSTERS

■ Ubisoft can't get enough of the Greek myths. First Assassin's Creed: Odyssey, now Gods & Monsters. And where Odyssey was a dark and brooding tale of war and vengeance, Gods & Monsters is an action RPG in the style of a Legend of Zelda, complete with gorgeous Greek scenery, legendary monsters, and a mysterious hero with the powers of the Greek gods. Love a sword and sandals epic? Jump on in.

46

BREAKING BEDE POKÉMON SWORD AND SHIELD

■ The latest Pokémon is full of drama, giant-sized creatures, and thrilling gym master battles, but if there's one thing we love more than anything else, it's putting your unbearable rival, Bede, back in his place. Each time he's beaten is sweeter than the last, even if the game can't bring itself to give him the fate he so richly deserves.

47

HAIL TO THE CHIEF HALO INFINITE

■ Halo 5: Guardians was fine, but it had one big problem: too much Locke and his Fireteam buddies, too little of the mighty Master Chief. Halo Infinite puts the spotlight back on everyone's favorite Spartan and on the kind of story, sci-fi settings, and epic battles that made Halo so exciting in the first place. This is the hero that gaming—and the Xbox—needs.

MEETING THE WILDLIFE
EVERWILD

49

■ A new game from Rare is always an occasion, and the studio followed up Sea of Thieves with this dazzling open world adventure. It's a game of wilderness and woodland teeming with fantasy wildlife, where—for once—the goal isn't to hunt and kill but to explore, discover, and preserve. It's not the first game where you'll walk the muddy paths of ancient lands, but Everwild's alive with mystery and wonder.

A NEW GENERATION
XBOX SERIES X AND
PLAYSTATION 5

50

■ There's nothing more exciting than a new console generation. Sure, we all know that the launch games might not be so great, and that the new hardware's going to cost a lot, but think about the new games and new experiences that we're going to get with the new machines. Imagine the worlds that game developers will be able to create, and the new characters we'll find inside them. There's still life in the old PS4 and Xbox One, but this is the dawn of a new console gaming era, and there's even more amazing stuff to come!

POKÉMON SWORD AND SHIELD

TRAIN YOUR WAY TO POKÉMON MASTERY

Pokémon Sword and Shield are the first "new" Pokémon games on Switch and, boy, has the wait been worthwhile. The two games bring us a whole new region to explore, new Pokémon to find and train, and a brilliant story that keeps you coming back for more.

This time, we're off to the Galar region, where our trainer hero and their bestie, Hop, are on a mission to write their own champion trainer legends. Can they beat the eight gym leaders and win the Champion Cup? Can they beat Hop's older brother, superstar trainer Leon, and all the other up-and-coming trainers who want to steal his crown? There's only one way to find out. Grab the game, search every corner of the region, and do your level best to catch 'em all!

QUICK TIPS:

GO HUNTING
■ Catch as many wild Pokémon as you can, and make sure you keep and train a range of different types in your team. Otherwise, you'll find you're weak in later battles.

MAKE CAMP
■ Camping, cooking, and playing with your Pokémon is a great way to build relationships and help them level up faster.

EVOLVE
■ Many Pokémon can evolve from one form into another once they level up, giving them more health and more powerful attacks. Try to train and evolve at least one Pokémon of each type. Even a cute-looking Pokémon like Grookey can become a fearsome warrior like Rillaboom!

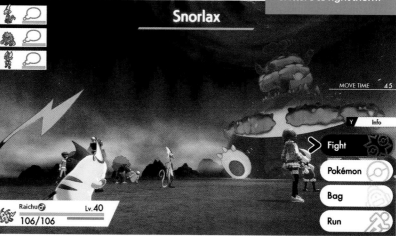

THE GALAR REGION

■ The latest Pokémon region is inspired by Britain, with country villages, steampunk cities, bustling harbor towns, and a busy metropolis based on London. Galar has 11 towns and cities connected by routes that run over hills, around lakes and ancient ruins, and through the mountains. It's swarming with secrets and wild Pokémon—and a place you'll love getting lost in.

THE WILD AREA

■ At the center of the region lies the massive Wild Area— the first open-world area in a Pokémon game— where you're free to hunt for wild Pokémon, fish, and find a lot of useful stuff.

■ You can also camp out and play with your Pokémon or treat them to a tasty meal. Build better friendships with your Pokémon and they'll fight even harder for you and earn extra XP, so it's well worth the effort!

■ The other thing you can do in the Wild Area is run Max Raids on the new supersized Dynamaxed Pokémon. You can raid solo with three CPU-controlled trainers or join up with other players online. The game even has built-in matchmaking to help you set this up!

■ There's lots to do in the Wild Area, but be careful: You can meet powerful Pokémon who'll be far too strong for you to battle. If they spot you, run away!

FAST FACT:

Pokémon Sword and Shield follow on from Pokémon: Let's Go, Pikachu! and Let's Go, Eevee!, both remakes of the GameBoy classic Pokémon Yellow from 1998.

DYNAMAXING

■ In the Max Raids and stadium battles, you'll be fighting Dynamaxed Pokémon: giant-sized Pokémon with super-strong attacks. Don't worry, though. You can temporarily Dynamax your own critters to fight them!

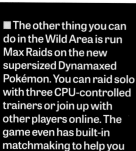

Snorlax

MOVE TIME   45

Y   Info

▶ Fight

Pokémon

Bag

Run

Raichu   Lv. 40
106/106

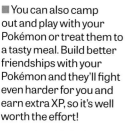

THE COMPETITION

You're not the only would-be champion out there. To make the grade, you'll have to beat these rivals.

MARNIE

■ Marnie is a rising star in the Galar region. She's followed everywhere by her own superfans. It's a shame that her Team Yell fans are a bunch of bully-boy punks—and that you're going to beat them when their antics go too far!

HOP

■ Hop might be your best friend, but at the start he sees you as just another tale in his own legend. You'll soon teach him the error of his ways, and he's got a few more lessons to learn before the story ends.

BEDE

■ Bede is the favorite of the chairman of the Galar Pokémon League, and as smug and rude as rivals come. He's always happy to stop and mock you and Hop—and he's just as quick with an excuse when you defeat him.

COMBAT CLASS

Struggling to win against wild Pokémon and rival trainers? Time to take your battle skills up a notch.

MATCH TYPE TO TYPE:

■ Each Pokémon belongs to a type, and each type is stronger or weaker against specific other types. For instance, Fire Pokémon are strong against Bug, Steel, Grass, and Ice Pokémon, but weak against Rock, Dragon, and Water. They also get hurt more by Rock, Water, and Ground attacks.

WATCH ATTACK EFFICIENCY:

■ When your Pokémon is battling another Pokémon, you'll see that some attacks are effective, very effective, or not effective against them. Fight more of them and you'll even see attacks labeled that way when you're choosing your next move. Learn which attacks work best against which Pokémon—and send out Pokémon with those attacks.

KEEP AN EYE ON YOUR HEALTH:

■ Always keep an eye on your health and carry plenty of potions, berries, and other healing items to keep your critters fighting fit. Revives are also handy for bringing back a fainted Pokémon— though you'd better heal them quickly if they haven't got much health!

SWORD VS SHIELD

■ What's the difference between Pokémon Sword and Shield? Well, for a start, each comes with exclusive Pokémon. In Shield, you might get Ponyta, Larvitar, and Croagunk, but not Sawk, Sirfecth'd, and Scraggy. The only way to get them all is to buy both games or trade Pokémon with other players.

X
Y — Info

> Fight

Pokémon

Bag

Run

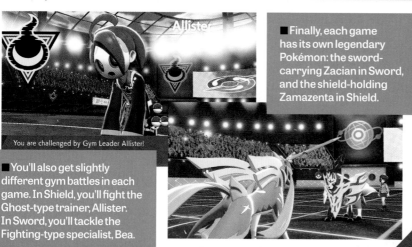

Allister

You are challenged by Gym Leader Allister!

■ You'll also get slightly different gym battles in each game. In Shield, you'll fight the Ghost-type trainer, Allister. In Sword, you'll tackle the Fighting-type specialist, Bea.

■ Finally, each game has its own legendary Pokémon: the sword-carrying Zacian in Sword, and the shield-holding Zamazenta in Shield.

SEE MORE OF GALAR!

■ You can take your Sword and Shield adventures even further with two downloadable expansions. Isle of Armor takes you to an island full of forests, bogs, and caves, with a weird training dojo and its own hardy wild Pokémon. The Crown Tundra has you journey to Galar's snow-topped mountains on a mission to investigate the frozen wilds. You'll need them both if you want to catch 'em all.

IT'S LIKE: POKÉMON: LET'S GO, PIKACHU!

■ It's a remake of one of the earliest Pokémon, but Let's Go, Pikachu! is still a great old-school Pokémon game. It even features some old favorites you won't find in the Galar region.

TRY: YO-KAI WATCH 4

■ This brilliant RPG series switches Pokémon little monsters for crazy ghosts and spectres—and it has amazing story lines and combat. It's out for both PS4 and Switch.

STAR WARS JEDI: FALLEN ORDER

RISE UP AGAINST THE EMPIRE AND BECOME A JEDI KNIGHT

Don't let the Jedi die out! Set between the prequel trilogy and the original Star Wars, this action-adventure follows a young Jedi apprentice, Cal, as he escapes the evil Empire and battles to restore the Jedi order.

Helped by a mysterious former Jedi Knight and hounded by the Empire's evil inquisitors, Cal needs to recover his forgotten Jedi powers and seek out the secrets of a lost civilization. Along the way, he'll explore new worlds and classic Star Wars locations, fighting monstrous creatures and stormtroopers all the way. You'll need awesome fighting and platforming skills to win through, in an epic that looks, feels, and sounds like a lost Star Wars movie.

QUICK TIPS:

MASTER THE LIGHTSABER
■ Just swinging your lightsaber around will get you nowhere. Learn how to block, evade, and time your attacks.

YOUR DROID BEST FRIEND
■ Your friendly droid, BD-1, can dish out healing "stims," scan the scenery for hints, and lead you to secret treasures. Keep an eye on him and don't forget to check his holomap.

CLEAR YOUR MIND
■ Meditating saves the game, and you can rest to heal and recharge your stims. Just watch out if you do, though. Your enemies respawn while you're relaxing!

USE THE FORCE

A JEDI KNIGHT'S WEAPON
■ Cal might not be a fully trained Jedi Knight, but he's no slouch with a lightsaber—and by unlocking skills you can unleash amazing moves.

BLOCK THE BLASTERS
■ Like any true Jedi, Cal can block blaster bolts with his lightsaber and even deflect them back at his stormtrooper enemies.

DEFY GRAVITY
■ Learn the ways of the force, and gravity won't hold you back. With practice, Cal can run along walls and make superhuman leaps through the air.

TAKE CONTROL OF TIME
■ Dodging missiles, racing along spinning platforms, running through dangerous machinery—all easy stuff when you can slow down time.

FAST FACT:
Fallen Order's most fearsome enemies—the Inquisitors—live to hunt down and kill the last Jedi. They answer to Darth Vader himself!

MIND OVER MATTER
■ You don't need to go hands-on to give something a good, hard shove. Why not pull objects toward you and toss stormtroopers around like toys?

IT'S LIKE: TOMB RAIDER
■ Cal's running, jumping, and climbing antics owe a lot to the adventures of Lara Croft, though it's more like older Tomb Raiders than her dark and gritty recent games.

TRY: STAR WARS: BATTLEFRONT II
■ Nothing captures the thrills of those massive Star Wars battles like this mighty multiplayer classic. Take the side of the Empire or the Rebellion in a galaxy far, far away.

MINECRAFT EARTH

AUGMENTED REALITY TECH PUTS MINECRAFT IN THE REAL WORLD

This is Minecraft, but maybe not as you know it. It's a Minecraft where your blocky creations pop into the real world around you—where you can build up from your kitchen table or go digging and discover a lava-filled dungeon right in the middle of your front yard.

It's also a Minecraft where you can share your adventures. With Minecraft Earth, you can not only wander around your neighborhood in search of useful resources, but meet up with friends and battle a castle full of skeletons in the park.

It all works thanks to the magic of augmented reality, or AR, which can superimpose digital images on top of a real-world image, and even have the two interact. You might have seen it in other games like Harry Potter: Wizards Unite or Pokémon GO, but here it brings Minecraft's blocky landscapes and mobs into life, right in front of your nose!

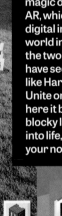

QUICK TIPS:

EXPLORE THE NEIGHBORHOOD
■ You'll need to collect resources to build in Minecraft Earth, and the best way to get them is to search around your neighborhood and tap on one whenever you find it.

FIND A FLAT SURFACE
■ You'll want a large, flat surface to put your virtual "build plates" on before you can start building. You might need to stand up to see your baseplate properly, and it helps if the area is brightly lit.

GEAR UP FOR ADVENTURE
■ It's worth crafting some equipment before you go off on an adventure. You want to be packing more than fists when you meet those underground mobs.

BUILD, BATTLE AND EXPLORE

BUILD
■ Build plates give you a simple scene to build on, including a small area of ground, trees, or buildings, and even some animals thrown in. You can add blocks and take them away, or add new stuff from your inventory.

EXPLORE
■ Once you've built something, you can take it outside and explore it, giant-sized, in View mode. You can walk all around your creation and even open doors or peer through windows and take a look inside.

JOIN THE ADVENTURE
■ It's not just about building, though. Go to certain spaces marked on your map and you're guaranteed an adventure. Each one gives you a virtual scene to discover, complete with treasures to be found and monsters to battle.

FIGHT THE MOBS
■ Some adventures are peaceful scenes with sheep and cows, but you might find a den of skeletons just inches under the ground of your local park—or a nest of venomous spiders!

IT'S LIKE:
POKEMON GO
■ In some ways, Minecraft Earth is the next step on from Pokémon GO, bringing a whole Minecraft world to life as well as its creatures.

TRY:
HARRY POTTER: WIZARDS UNITE
■ Take a trip to the wizarding world in another top augmented reality game. Search for magical creatures and battle dark magic in challenging fortresses with your spell-casting friends.

FAST FACT:
Tappable resources are a big thing in Minecraft Earth. When a test of the game launched in Japan, fans rode the bullet train to hoover them up at lightning speed—and nearly broke the system.

FINAL FANTASY VII REMAKE

CLOUD'S COMEBACK IS THE STUFF OF LEGENDS

We've had plenty of awesome remakes and remasters, but Final Fantasy VII Remake is the most eagerly awaited of them all. The 1997 original was the first Japanese RPG to break through in the States, and its incredible story and stunning cutscenes left a huge impression on a whole gaming generation. But this remake isn't just about nostalgia—it's about taking an all-time classic and giving it a modern style, then going even deeper into the much-loved tale.

In fact, this is only the first part of Final Fantasy VII, with a second part coming soon (we hope). You might complain that all we get is the first chunk of the story, set in the industrial city of Midgar, but Square Enix has packed a whole Final Fantasy game's worth of depth and detail into the episode, massively expanding on what we saw in the original. More Cloud, more Aerith, more Tifa, Barrett, and the Turks. If you're looking for an epic adventure, this is the gaming event of the year.

Cloud   HP 484/1026

QUICK TIPS:

ACTIVE BATTLES
■ Final Fantasy VII Remake has an all-new battle system, where you move and attack in real-time, but can slow down the action to use magic and abilities when you fill up the Active Time Battle gauge. Make the most of it to heal your party or hit your toughest enemy with a fatal blow.

SWITCH HEROES
■ You can switch between your heroes while in battle, giving you access to their attacks and spells. Finding a fight is going nowhere? Try another hero and a different approach.

SUMMON IN SOME HELP
■ Summonings are back, so you can call in old friends like Ifrit and Shiva to lay the smack down on your biggest foes. You can have only one active summoning per character, though, so think carefully about which ones you choose.

HEROES AND VILLAINS

CLOUD STRIFE

■ Final Fantasy VII's protagonist is a mercenary swordsman with a dark past and a bad attitude. Can his friends help him become the hero that the world needs him to be?

AERITH GAINSBOROUGH

■ This upbeat flower seller joins Cloud in the fight against Shinra, but with her magical powers is she more than she appears?

TIFA LOCKHART

■ Cloud's childhood friend is a member of Avalanche—a resistance group fighting against the Shinra corporation. She's a tough martial artist with some mighty special moves.

FAST FACT:
Cloud's Buster Sword is one of gaming's most legendary weapons. In real life, it would be too heavy to be usable!

BARRETT WALLACE
■ The leader of Avalanche wants to prevent Shinra's continued exploitation of the planet's life force, and will do whatever it takes to save the world. Don't mess with his bullet-spitting gun-arm.

SEPIROTH
■ One of gaming's greatest villains, Sepiroth is a troubled soul with superhuman abilities and a seven-foot sword. His desire for vengeance knows no end.

PRESIDENT SHINRA

■ The evil head of the Shinra Electric Power Company. He dreams of rebuilding Midgar city as a high-tech heaven for Shinra to rule, and doesn't care about the human or environmental costs.

IT'S LIKE:
FINAL FANTASY XV
■ Every Final Fantasy is different, but Final Fantasy XV is widely seen as a return to form. It's got a great story, lovable characters, and an incredible world-spanning adventure.

TRY: TALES OF BERSERIA
■ The Tales series isn't as well known as Final Fantasy, but Tales of Berseria is a great Japanese RPG with a strong heroine, inventive quests, and a brilliant, unpredictable tale to tell.

LEGO STAR WARS: THE SKYWALKER SAGA

ALL NINE MOVIES IN ONE BRICKBUSTER OF A GAME

The last time the LEGO games tackled Star Wars, they focused on *The Force Awakens*, but with Episodes VIII and IX now out of the way we're looking at the whole nine movie saga. That's right. All the heroes and villains and the most iconic scenes are here, covering everything from *Episode I: The Phantom Menace* to *Episode IX: The Rise of Skywalker*.

No wonder this is the most ambitious LEGO project yet, with over 200 playable characters to unlock and five levels per movie, which you can play in any order.

Cleverly, the locations change depending on when you visit, so that Jabba's sail barge will be floating over the sands of Tatooine if you visit during the original trilogy, but not if you visit during the prequel era. We also get more realistic worlds to roam around. Your plastic heroes' feet will even get dusted with snow or encrusted with swamp mud when you're speeding around Hoth or Dagobah.

Throw in changes to make the combat more exciting, along with some brilliant space battles, and we think this is the best LEGO Star Wars of them all!

QUICK TIPS:

TAKE AIM
■ This is the first LEGO game where you can aim a blaster. Try blasting away at different body parts to see what happens.

USE YOUR COMBOS
■ Previous LEGO games had simple fighting moves, but in The Skywalker Saga you can pull off different combos, depending on your current character. Check out what the different Jedi and Sith characters can do with their lightsabers.

RETURN OF THE JEDI
■ To track down all the different characters and vehicles, you'll need to keep exploring the levels using different Star Wars stars. If you can't get past an obstacle now, maybe you can come back later playing someone else.

ICONIC SCENES

GEONOSIS
■ Replay some of the standout scenes of *Attack of the Clones*, taking on Count Dooku's battle droids and the fiendish Jango Fett.

TATOOINE
■ Hang out with the Jawas and meet up with the young Luke Skywalker, then return to rescue Han from Jabba the Hut and the Sarlacc Pit.

ENDOR
■ Help the Ewoks battle Imperial forces and bring down the new Death Star's shields before the Rebel ships can be destroyed.

STARKILLER BASE
■ Rey and Kylo Ren duel for the first time as the Resistance fights to destroy the New Order's planet-wrecking weapon.

PASAANA
■ As Poe and Finn work to track down the lost Sith wayfinder, Rey finds herself facing Kylo Ren once more. You might remember this bit from the trailer!

FAST FACT:
The first LEGO Star Wars playsets came out in 1999 along with *Episode I: The Phantom Menace*. Almost 700 sets have been released over the last 21 years.

IT'S LIKE: LEGO MARVEL SUPER HEROES 2
■ Everyone has their favorite LEGO game, but this could be the high point of the series. It has a massive roster of Marvel heroes and villains, and a universe-spanning campaign.

TRY: LEGO HARRY POTTER COLLECTION
■ There's another LEGO title covering an epic saga, bringing in all the magic of the movies from *The Sorcerer's Stone* to *The Deathly Hallows*.

MINECRAFT DUNGEONS

TIRED OF DUNGEON CRAWLERS – THIS ONE'S A CREEPER!

Looking for a new kind of Minecraft adventure? Find some friends and delve underground. The latest Minecraft hit is a classic dungeon crawler in the style of Diablo and Titan Quest, only this one has Minecraft's brilliant blocky graphics, and all the critters and mobs you know and love. Whacking monsters, grabbing loot, and upgrading your gear is the name of the game, and you can do it solo or with up to three friends. It's good online, but even better in old-school couch co-op.

There's a story—a disgruntled villager finds a magic orb, turns evil, and brings others under his sway—but you don't need to worry about it too much. The joy of Minecraft Dungeons lies in exploring its maze-like areas, fighting zombies, skeletons, and creepers, then finding new and more incredible enchanted weapons with which to menace even tougher monsters. Your skills will be challenged as you face hordes of fiendish foes—and their bosses—but you've got what it takes to win!

FAST FACT:

Minecraft Dungeons was originally designed as a 3DS game, but the developers loved it so much that they expanded their ideas and moved the game onto Xbox One, PS4, Switch, and PC.

CRAFT A HERO

PLATE ARMOR

- +0 health
- 20% chance to negate hits
- 20% damage reduction
- 10% move speed

Plate armor turns even the most average soldier into a fortress but comes with reduced mobility.

SALVAGE

Enchantments

HIGHLAND ARMOR

- +133 health
- Gains Speed after Dodge
- 20% damage reduction
- +15% melee damage

The educated elders of the Ender days claimed that this armor was built from the scales of a dragon.

Enchantments

■ Unlike other dungeon crawlers, Minecraft Dungeons doesn't have classes. Any hero can use any weapon and wear any armor, and there aren't any abilities only for warriors or wizards to use.

■ That doesn't mean you can't build a hero to match the way you want to play. Start with the armor. A suit of plate armor will make you tough in combat, but also slow. Other armor sets will be lighter, so faster to move and faster to attack.

■ Weapons make a big difference, too. As well as melee weapons, like swords, scythes, axes, and hammers, you'll find ranged weapons, like a trusty crossbow or a bow and arrow.

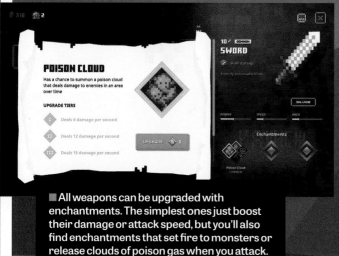

POISON CLOUD

Has a chance to summon a poison cloud that deals damage to enemies in an area over time

UPGRADE TIERS

- I. Deals 6 damage per second
- II. Deals 12 damage per second
- III. Deals 18 damage per second

UPGRADE

SWORD

- 30-48 damage

A sturdy and reliable blade

SALVAGE

POWER   SPEED   AREA

Enchantments

Poison Cloud
COMMON

NIGHTMARE'S BITE

- 22-50 damage
- Spawns Poison Clouds
- Dual Wield

The twin blades of Nightmare's Bite drip with deadly venom, still potent after all these years.

POWER   SPEED   AREA

Enchantments

■ All weapons can be upgraded with enchantments. The simplest ones just boost their damage or attack speed, but you'll also find enchantments that set fire to monsters or release clouds of poison gas when you attack.

■ Some monsters and chests will also drop unique or special magic weapons, which have their own perks even before they're enchanted. Watch out for these!

QUICK TIPS:

RAID THE PIGGY BANK
■ Watch out for the speedy little porker with the chest on its back. It's carrying its weight in precious loot!

USE THE ARTEFACTS
■ Magical artefacts, like the various totems, can turn the tide of a tricky battle. You'll find totems that can shield you from monsters or heal you while you're fighting.

STOP THE NECROMANCER
■ This nameless horror resurrects dead mobs. Until you slay him, they'll keep coming back for more!

FIGHT TOGETHER

■ Minecraft Dungeons is fun if you're playing solo, but it's even better if you're playing with friends. You can play online or in a couch co-op mode on one PC or console. We love couch co-op, even if it means you all have to stick together. There's no split-screen in this one.

■ Players can drop in and out of the action as they like, so you can join in a game halfway through or leave if your mom is calling you down to have your dinner. The game adjusts its difficulty, so when you add new players you'll still get a decent challenge!

■ Cleverly, the game reserves specific items for you when you kill the monsters, so you don't have to worry about one of your group rushing through the level and grabbing all of the best stuff.

IT'S LIKE: TORCHLIGHT 2
■ Here's another dungeon crawler that doesn't take itself too seriously. You can now play this massive, bright, and enjoyable adventure on everything from PC to Switch.

TRY: DRAGON QUEST BUILDERS 2
■ This offshoot of the classic Japanese RPG series mixes Minecraft-style building with exploration and adventure. There's a touch of Minecraft in its blocky graphics, too.

BECOME A DUNGEONS MASTER

KEEP EXPLORING

■ Minecraft Dungeons uses clever "procedural generation" techniques to build a new dungeon for every level of the game each time you play. While some crucial areas might be the same, you can replay the same dungeon another day and find new rooms, new monsters, and new secrets to explore.

USE THE MAP

■ You can call up a dungeon map at the tap of a button and it makes it much, much easier to find your way around.

FLIP THE SWITCH

■ See a switch or a footplate? Try to activate it. You might open up a hidden area or disarm or disarm a deadly trap.

FEAR THE CREEPER

■ Most of the monsters will be familiar from regular Minecraft, and have the same attacks and abilities. Zombies will try to surround you, then claw and bite you, while hordes of spiders will rush in for a chomp. Creepers will try to get close, then blow up in your face. Don't let them get anywhere near!

WORK AS A TEAM

■ If you're playing in a duo or a group, look after your teammates. You can revive them if they're killed or use totems to protect them—and you might need them to do the same for you.

HALO INFINITE
THE STORY SO FAR

It's been five years since Halo 5: Guardians. Do you need a catch-up on where we are?

HALO 1 TO 3

■ In Halo: Combat Evolved, the Master Chief—a biologically enhanced super soldier—prevents the alien Covenant from unleashing a fast-breeding parasitic organism, the Flood, from a mysterious artificial ring world, the Halo.

■ But humanity isn't safe. Urged on by fanatical leaders, the Prophet of Truth and the Prophet of Regret, the Covenant attack Earth and attempt to activate a new Delta Halo, but are foiled once again by the Master Chief, a rogue Covenant warrior, the Arbiter, and the Master Chief's ally, Miranda Keyes.

■ By the end of Halo 3, the Master Chief and the Arbiter have stopped the Prophet of Truth from activating all the Halo rings hidden around the galaxy—a move that would have doomed not just mankind, but all living things. However, the Master Chief is left stranded in deep space with Cortana. His last words before going into cryo-sleep are "wake me when you need me."

HALO 4

■ The Master Chief awakens to find himself on the UNSC Infinity, years after the events of Halo 3. The Infinity is on its way to a new world, Requiem, where the Diadact—one of the ancient Forerunners that created the Halo rings—has woken up after centuries of sleep.

■ The Diadact hates humanity and plans to use an army of Promethean warriors and a device, the Composer, to enslave the human race.

■ The Master Chief battles to stop him, while also trying desperately to save Cortana, whose AI personality is starting to deteriorate after years of service. Helped by another Forerunner, the Librarian, the Master Chief defeats the Diadact. Cortana sacrifices herself to protect him as they destroy the Composer.

HALO 5: GUARDIANS

■ While fighting Covenant scavengers on a captured research ship, the Master Chief has a vision of Cortana activating an enormous alien machine. With his Spartan squad, Blue Team, he follows her to the planet of Meridian, but is pursued by a second Spartan fireteam, Osiris, led by ex-spy Jameson Locke.

■ Locke's team believe that Cortana is manipulating the Master Chief, and discover that she's working with a Forerunner AI, the Warden Eternal, to combine the powers of all the AIs in the galaxy and take it over. Cortana plans to ensure peace in the galaxy using gigantic Forerunner machines: the Guardians.

■ Fighting together on a Forerunner world, Blue Team and Osiris are unable to stop the crazed Cortana, but escape on the UNSC Infinity to fight another day. As the game ends, we see a new Halo ring orbiting above a green planet.

FAST FACT:

Halo Infinite uses new graphics technology and has a different art style than the last two games, aimed at bringing the series back to the style of the original Halo.

HALO INFINITE

■ The new game finds the Master Chief drifting near-lifelessly in space, where he's discovered by a stranded dropship orbiting a shattered Halo ring. The pilot of the dropship manages to awaken the Master Chief, but seconds later they're attacked by a mysterious force. It's time to return to the fight!

■ Who is their attacker? Where is this Halo? What does this have to do with Cortana and her plans? There's only one way to find out: play Halo Infinite.

SUPER-CO

The Xbox Series X and PlayStation 5 take us into a new world of gaming

■ The next generation of gaming consoles is nearly here. Seven years on from the launch of the Xbox One and the PS4, we have two new powerhouse games machines to take us into gaming's awesome future.

■ These consoles have the processing power to create even bigger, better game worlds, with more believable characters and amazing real-world physics. They give game developers the graphics technology they need to bring those worlds to life, using techniques that we've only seen before in computer-generated special effects and animation.

■ They use new storage technology that will cut down your loading times and deliver these epic game worlds, and new sound technologies that will transform the way we play. Excited? You should be. Read on!

FAST FACT:
Both the PS5 and the Xbox Series X use chips designed by one manufacturer, AMD. However, both Sony and Microsoft customize their chips to add their own "secret sauce."

PLAYSTATION 5 HARDWARE FEATURES

3D AUDIO SOUND

HAPTICS / ADAPTIVE TRIGGERS

ULTRA-HIGH SPEED SSD

HARDWARE-BASED RAY TRACING

ULTRA HD BLU-RAY

NSOLES

PROCESSING POWER

■ The old consoles had surprisingly weak processors (or CPUs in computer jargon). While these were based on the same basic technology you would find in your PC or laptop, they ran at much slower speeds and held game developers back.

■ The processors in the new consoles are different. They're based on chip manufacturer AMD's latest Zen2 technology, and each one has eight cores—eight mini processors inside the chip that run the code for your games—which run at much higher speeds. What's more, each core can run two lots of code at once, which means it can get double the work done, faster.

■ All that work also uses the console's RAM, which stores all the code the processor is working through and the results of all the millions of calculations that it's

doing every second. Both consoles have double the amount of RAM of the last-generation consoles and that RAM runs at faster speeds. This means the processor isn't kept waiting for the information it needs to get things done.

■ What does this mean in games? For a start, bigger worlds with more realistic physics, so you can, say, fire your cannons at a pirate ship and see it explode in dozens of animated, flying chunks of timber.

■ Or how about worlds full of more believable people and animals, all getting on with their everyday lives, or battles where you're fighting alongside an army against an army, and each soldier can fight intelligently?

■ You might have seen some of this stuff before, but never with this detail and never at such a massive scale. Next-generation games should be amazing!

SPEEDY STORAGE

■ All the code, art and sound that makes up a game has to be stored somewhere, and the faster the processor and graphics processor can get it, the better. The old consoles relied on the same magnetic hard drive storage we've been using in PCs for over 30 years, but the new ones have swapped it for what we call solid-state storage.

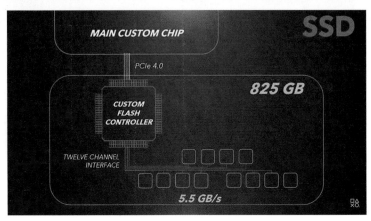

MAIN CUSTOM CHIP

SSD

PCIe 4.0

825 GB

CUSTOM FLASH CONTROLLER

TWELVE CHANNEL INTERFACE

5.5 GB/s

■ It also means that the new consoles can do some really clever stuff with the games you're playing. For instance, the Xbox Series X will be able to keep several games, complete with saves games, in a standby mode at once, and let you get back to playing any one of them in an instant!

■ All these games will use a lot of storage space, but both consoles allow you to expand it. The Xbox Series X will have special plug-in expansion units, while it's going to be a simple upgrade with the PS5.

■ Solid-state storage is what you would find in your smartphone, tablet or modern laptop, and it's much, much faster than the old magnetic stuff.

■ This means a lot more than just faster loading times. Sony has explained how the revolutionary storage tech inside the PS5 lets game developers build epic games with incredible amounts of detail. They can then feed the data needed to the processor and graphics processor straight from storage as the player moves. Even while you're turning your head to look at a distant landscape, the storage could be sending through the data needed to show what you would see far away.

■ Sony has even shown off a version of Marvel's Spider-Man where the SSD technology allows Spidey to swing through the streets of Manhattan at the speed of a fighter jet, without a single pause!

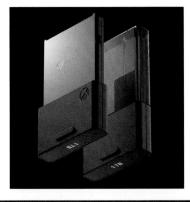

NEXT-LEVEL GRAPHICS

■ It's no surprise that both new consoles have more powerful graphics processors than ever before: Microsoft says that the Xbox Series X will be four times more powerful than the current Xbox One X.

■ Both consoles have the hardware to run games at a silky smooth 60 frames per second on a modern 4K TV, with new effects and more detailed textures. This should make your games look more lifelike than they ever have before—or closer to the kind of computer-generated animation you'd expect from a Pixar movie.

■ Think that your current games look great? Games on the Xbox Series X and PS5 will knock your socks off and make you drop your jaw to the floor.

■ One of the big new features of both next-generation consoles is ray-tracing. This is a clever graphics technique used in 3D art, movies, and animation, that simulates how light behaves as it bounces off different surfaces in the real world.

Ray Tracing On
Technical Demo

Ray Tracing Off

■ You'll see it used a lot in future games to create more realistic lighting, produce amazing metal surfaces, or water where you can see the whole scene around you reflected, exactly like you would in real life. Take a look at it in action in a special experimental version of Minecraft running on the Xbox Series X. Who knew the old blockbuster could look this good?

CONTROLLERS

■ The new Xbox Series X and Dual Sense controllers aren't hugely different from the old ones on the surface, but there's some cool new tech underneath. The Dual Sense uses a new physical feedback technology that replaces the old rumble with more convincing vibration effects, a bit like the clever HD Rumble technology used in the Nintendo Switch. It also has a similar technology built into the triggers, so that they'll give your fingers more or less resistance, depending on whether you're pressing down on the gas pedal in a NASCAR vehicle or pulling the trigger on a sci-fi gun.

■ The Xbox Series X controller is close to the already brilliant Xbox One pad, but it uses a new wireless technology designed to cut down the tiny delay between you pressing the button and your character reacting on the screen. This is super-important in competitive eSports and tough action games. It might even give your gaming skills a boost!

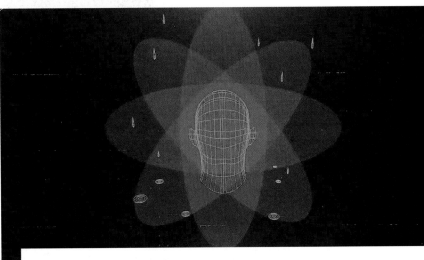

Its eight-core processor runs at a maximum 3.5GHz and can turn its speed up and down, depending on the game.

Its custom 36-unit RDNA2 graphics processor runs at 2.23GHz and can process over 10 trillion instructions a second—over five times as many as the PS4 and over twice as many as the PS4 Pro.

With 16GB of GDDR6 RAM, it has double the memory of the PS4 and PS4 Pro, running at higher speeds.

Its 1TB SSD gives you the same storage space as the PS4 Pro, but it's one of the fastest SSDs ever made and designed especially for the PS5.

It's the first PlayStation console to have a 4K UHD Blu-ray drive.

SUPER SURROUND SOUND

■ In games, the sound never gets as much attention as the graphics. Yet good sound can transform a game, making spooky games even spookier and action games even more exciting. It can also improve your gameplay, because you can use the sound to work out where enemies might be hiding or even let you know that there's a battle up ahead.

■ The PS5 and Xbox Series X aim to take this to another level. The PS5 has a brand-new sound processor called the Tempest Engine, which has been built to produce amazing 3D surround sound. It's designed to work with TV speakers and headphones, as well as more expensive surround sound systems, and it uses some clever technology to put hundreds of different sounds in the space all around you.

■ This won't just convince your ears that you're really in the game world, but make it even easier to work out that, for instance, a group of monsters is chasing you. They're directly behind you—and they're getting closer every second!

■ The Xbox Series X hasn't got the same kind of sound hardware, but it will support the same Dolby Atmos technology used in cinemas and home theater setups to create similar effects. That's music to our ears!

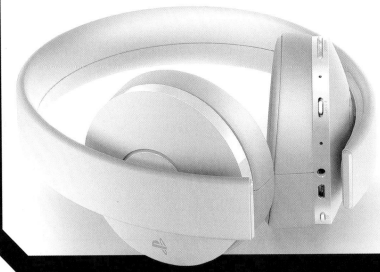

NEW GAMES
(AND OLD FAVORITES)

■ The Xbox Series X and PS5 are launching with some big games. Some, like Halo: Infinite, Gods and Monsters, Fall of Tsushima, and the new Assassin's Creed, are also launching on the existing Xbox One and PS4 consoles, but they'll look even better running on the new hardware. Others, like the PS5 exclusive, Godfall, are designed to take advantage of the new consoles' graphics power.

■ Cleverly, Sony and Microsoft have made it easier for developers to produce games that will run across two console generations, but we'll still see some games in the future that will only run on PS5, or that won't give you quite the same experience if you're playing on an older Xbox One S or One X.

■ One bonus of the similar hardware, though, is that it's going to be easier to get your existing games up and running on the new machines. Nearly all Xbox One games will run faster and in 4K on the Xbox Series X, and Microsoft even has some clever technology that will add new graphics features to your existing

games automatically. This could make them look almost as good as next-generation games. Gears 5, for instance, gets enhanced mist and HDR lighting effects, thanks to Microsoft's new tech.

■ The PS5 will also run nearly all PS4 games, so your existing game collection won't go to waste. In fact, your old games should look and run better than they ever have before!

XBOX SERIES X: THE NUMBERS

Its eight-core processor runs at 3.8GHz.

Its custom 52-unit RDNA2 graphics processor can process over 12 trillion instructions a second— eight times as many as the original Xbox One.

With 16GB of GDDR6 RAM, it has double the memory of the Xbox One running at higher speeds.

Its 1TB SSD gives you the same storage as the Xbox One's HDD, but running a whole lot faster.

Like the Xbox One S and Xbox One X, it has a 4K UHD Blu-ray drive.

ox Series X

SUPER SMASH BROS. ULTIMATE

NINTENDO'S CLASSIC BEAT 'EM UP KEEPS GETTING STRONGER

Think Super Smash Bros. Ultimate couldn't get any better? Think again. Since launch, we've had six updates adding new features to the game, along with five fantastic DLC fighters representing some of the greatest video games ever!

This takes the total number of fighters all the way up to 75. Sure, some are just variations on the same hero or villain, but that's still a lot of stars and moves to come to grips with. Throw in nine different play modes, some both single-player and multiplayer, and this isn't a game you're going to get tired of any time soon.

Get in there, explore the newest modes and fighters, and find out why Super Smash Bros. Ultimate keeps smashing it out of the park!

QUICK TIPS:

CUT THE COUNTDOWN

■ Looking to unlock new characters faster? Normally the game has a minimum 10-minute cooldown before a new challenger appears, but you can reset this just by quitting your current game mode and coming back or trying a different mode.

USE YOUR SHIELD

■ Raise your shield if you don't want to get smashed around the stage. That shrinking bubble can't hold off all the damage, but it will soak up the worst of it.

MASTER COMEBACK MOVES

■ If you get launched off a platform, don't give up. Each character has a recovery move (press B and Up at the same time), which can be used to get back into the action.

HOME RUN
■ One of our favorite new features is the return of the classic Home Run Contest mode. You have a sandbag and just 10 seconds to do as much damage as possible. Do enough, grab the bat, then smash that sandbag through the sky. How far can you make it go?

FAST FACT:
Super Smash Bros. Ultimate has sold nearly 16 million copies around the world, making it the bestselling fighting game ever.

THE NEW SMASH STARS

HERO
■ The Luminary from Dragon Quest XI puts in a great guest appearance. He has some hard-hitting combos and a real height advantage, plus a shield that can block projectiles. He also comes with alternate outfits based on other classic Dragon Quest games.

BANJO-KAZOOIE
■ The duo from Rare's classic platform games work together as a single heavy fighter. They're slow to move until they get going, but surprisingly speedy once they do, and they've got some really nasty jab and smash attacks. Just watch out for their weak knockout moves.

TERRY BOGARD
■ Terry's on loan from the legendary Fatal Fury and King of Fighters series and, man, does he know how to fight! He's got some brutal flying kicks, punches, throws, and uppercuts, making it easy to launch his enemies off the ground and high into the air.

IT'S LIKE:
STREET FIGHTER 30TH ANNIVERSARY COLLECTION
■ Looking for a classic beat 'em up? This collection bundles in the games that helped define the fighting game genre.

TRY: ARMS
■ Nintendo's revolutionary 3D fighting game wasn't as successful as it should have been, but it's as exciting and inventive as a Super Smash Bros. or Splatoon.

HOLLOW KNIGHT: SILKSONG

EXPLORE A NEW INSECT UNDERWORLD IN THE STUNNING HOLLOW KNIGHT SEQUEL

QUICK TIPS:

SPRING INTO ACTION

■ Hornet is slightly larger, faster, and more acrobatic than the knight of the original game. Master her different jump, dash, and aerial attack moves if you want to make it to the top.

FIND THE MASK SHARDS

■ Each area hides pieces of a mask in secret or hard-to-reach areas. Track these down, collect four, and you'll get another mask on your health meter, helping you to survive.

BEAT THE BOSSES

■ Each boss has their own killer moves, requiring quick responses and a careful strategy. Just rushing in and hacking away with Hornet's blade is going to get you absolutely nowhere.

Hollow Knight is one of the great surprise indie hits of the last few years. Set in a strange and magical world of insect fantasy, it's gathered fans on every system it's appeared on, partly thanks to its beautiful, haunted, hand-painted graphics. Hollow Knight: Silksong has the same star quality, but with a new lead and creepy-crawly underworld to dive into.

You might recognize our new hero. The game begins with Hornet, Princess Protector of Hallownest, captured, caged, and taken to a mysterious new kingdom. She escapes and makes a journey to the highest peak of the realm, passing from the mossy caverns at the bottom through coral forests, chambers full of lava, and shining, golden insect citadels. She faces new enemies and makes new friends, but why was she taken and what evil has corrupted this land? Draw your blade and keep moving upward to find out!

NOTES IN THE SONG

MOSS GROTTO:
■ The first and lowest level of the kingdom is a beautiful moss-covered cave system crawling with weird-looking grubs.

FAST FACT:

Silksong started off as a DLC expansion for Hollow Knight, but grew so big and ambitious that it became a sequel.

FORGE DAUGHTER:
■ This helpful new character will build you new weapons, traps, and armor, as long as you've got the materials and rosary beads to buy them.

LACE:
■ This cruel boss wants to save you from your suffering—by skewering you with her sword. She's fast, precise, and deadly, so treat her with respect!

DEEP DOCKS:
■ This hostile underground area features lakes and chutes of lava along with evil creatures who want to see Hornet crushed.

HUNTER QUEEN CARMELITA:
■ Queen of the red ant people, you'll battle this boss inside a theater packed with opera-loving insects. Watch out for her dual spinning blades and spikey ground pound!

IT'S LIKE: GUACAMELEE!
■ Guacamelee! was one of the first in a new wave of "metroidvania" games, where players explored complex 2D worlds. With a lovable Mexican theme, it's still one of the best.

TRY: BLOODSTAINED: RITUAL OF THE NIGHT
■ Bloodstained is a love letter to Castlevania, developed by one of its creators. Castlevania inspired both Hollow Knight and the whole metroidvania style.

MARVEL'S AVENGERS

MARVEL'S MIGHTIEST HEROES ASSEMBLE FOR ONE AMAZING GAME

Sure, these aren't the Avengers you remember from the Marvel movies, but the new Avengers game is every bit as exciting. Square Enix and Crystal Dynamics, the team behind the Tomb Raider reboots, have crafted a whole new superhero story, where a catastrophe in San Francisco results in the team disbanding.

With no heroes to protect the world, governments start to rely on a mysterious military mega-corporation, AIM.

Enter Ms. Marvel, Kamala Khan. Five years on from the end of the Avengers, she becomes convinced that AIM is up to no good. As she can't take them on alone, she decides it's time to get the old team back together. You

recruit the ex-Avengers, go on missions, investigate AIM facilities, and stop the bad guys in their tracks. It all makes one incredible action-adventure, where you can play solo or team up with friends to fight in the shoes of seven favorite Marvel heroes. If the time since *Avengers: Endgame* has left you missing the classic lineup, you'll find them all in the game.

A GROUP OF REMARKABLE PEOPLE

CAPTAIN AMERICA
■ Steve Rogers has superhuman strength and speed, hard-hitting combat moves, and a shield he can throw around.

BLACK WIDOW
■ Natasha Romanoff doesn't have superpowers, but don't let that fool you: She's a highly trained athlete and super-spy with the skills to take on AIM's troops.

THOR
■ The God of Thunder can fly, discharge lightning on command, and whack AIM goons around with his mighty hammer.

FAST FACT:
There's no Chris Evans or Robert Downey Jr., but Crystal Dynamic has assembled a heroic team of voice talent. Troy Baker and Nolan North are games industry legends, while Travis Willingham has played Thor before in several Marvel animated series.

HULK
■ Of course, Hulk smashes, but he's also strong enough to throw tanks and troops around like toys. He's also got some brilliant Hulk-style wall-running and jumping moves to get around.

QUICK TIPS:

FIGHT SMART
■ Each Avenger has their own style of movement and their own style of fighting, so remember to play to their strengths. Use Cap's shield and Ms. Marvel's long reach. And remember that Black Widow can't soak up damage like the Hulk.

UPGRADE
■ Remember to upgrade your heroes between missions. You can choose which powers and abilities to boost, and customize your heroes for the way you like to play.

TEAM UP
■ Experience and upgrades from the multiplayer missions carry over into the single-player campaign. If you're struggling solo, find some friends, level up, and come back ready for the battle.

IRON MAN
■ Why fight on the ground when you can take to the skies, using rockets and repulsor rays to take on the world's biggest threats?

MS. MARVEL
■ One-time superhero fangirl, now inspiration behind the new Avengers, Kamala Khan can extend her limbs, change forms, and alter her appearance at will.

CUSTOMIZE YOUR HEROES

■ Each hero has a range of different outfits, including classic costumes from the comics and new ones designed just for the game.

■ As you play, you find and earn resources that allow you to unlock new gear. Each item of equipment gives your hero new perks and powers.

■ You also earn skill points you can spend to upgrade your superpowers and abilities. Different combos, attacks, and weapons open up as the game goes on, making your heroes even more formidable.

AVENGERS ASSEMBLE

■ Marvel's Avengers has two types of missions. Campaign missions advance the story, taking one or a small group of heroes somewhere where they'll fight AIM forces, take on supervillains, and take the next step in saving the world from evil. These missions are packed with the kind of battles and spectacular action sequences you'd expect from an Avengers game.

AMERICAN SOUTHWEST
OPERATION REASSEMBLE

BREAKOUT
CAMPAIGN MISSION

18
Normal

Dr Pym has identified the location of an AIM holding facility. The Avengers need to go in and break out captured Resistance fighters before they're moved to a new location.

REWARDS

GUARANTEED REWARD
Rare Gear

PERFORMANCE BONUS
Random Gear

Select Mission

Select Difficulty

■ You can tune the difficulty level and, while the combat features special moves and combos, it also involves a lot of follow-the-prompt quick time events. You can play along with someone who hasn't got elite gaming skills—like your dad!

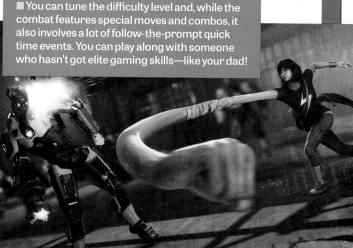

■ Warzone missions are designed to be played by up to four players online, putting a team of Avengers against a legion of AIM troops, tougher villains, or giant AIM dreadbots. The threats are higher, but so are the rewards: You can earn rare gear to upgrade your hero with.

IT'S LIKE: MARVEL'S SPIDER-MAN
■ Marvel's Spider-Man gives you a similar alternate take on a classic Marvel hero, working outside the cinematic universe. It's also one of the best superhero games ever.

TRY: MONSTER HUNTER
■ Looking for another game where you can work together to battle fearsome foes? Team up with fellow hunters, craft your own weapons and armor, then bring down ferocious brutes.

LUIGI'S MANSION 3

RID A HAUNTED HOTEL OF ITS GHOSTLY RESIDENTS

Almost nobody looks as nervous as Luigi—and this time the younger Mario bro has plenty of reasons to shiver. He's stuck on his lonesome in a creepy hotel, with his mushroom kingdom friends imprisoned and ghosts everywhere you look. Luckily, Luigi's equipped to clean things up, using Professor E. Gadd's latest Poltergust G-00 vacuum cleaner to suck up the spectres, and save his nearest and dearest from disaster.

With 17 floors to explore, there's a lot to discover, each themed level getting stranger as the game goes on. What other hotel packs in pirate ships or scary tombs? Plus, each room is crammed with secrets to uncover with the aid of E. Gadd's ingenious contraption. Looking for a game with shocks, frights, and ghostly delights? The guy in green has you covered.

QUICK TIPS:

USE THE FLASHLIGHT
■ Luigi's flashlight doesn't just light the way—a quick blast freezes most ghosts in their tracks. This makes them much easier to suck up.

CHECK THE SCENERY
■ Treasure could be hiding on every shelf and behind every curtain. Use the Poltergust to investigate and move everything you can.

FIND THE GEMS
■ Each floor of the hotel has six special gems to collect, though you'll need a sharp eye and a brilliant brain if you want Luigi to get them all.

POLTERGUST POWER!

SUCK AND SLAM:
■ Want to get rid of ghosts? Suck them, tilt the left stick in the opposite direction, then hammer A when prompted to slam them on the ground!

BLOW:
■ You can also set the Poltergust to blow with a squeeze of the ZL trigger—handy when you need to get a fan spinning or blow something light around the room.

BURST:
■ A quick blast of air from the Poltergust sends Luigi flying upward. It's no jetpack, but it will get him over some obstacles without taking damage.

IT'S LIKE: LUIGI'S MANSION: DARK MOON
■ Luigi's last haunted house adventure was a Nintendo 3DS classic, and still well worth exploring if you can get your hands on a 2DS or 3DS.

FAST FACT:
The original Luigi's Mansion wasn't the first game where Luigi was the star. He also took the central role in Mario is Missing!, a geography-themed game from 1993.

GOOIGI:
■ Click the right-stick and the green goo becomes a remote-controlled Luigi clone, capable of squeezing through barriers that hold back the real Luigi.

TRY: GHOSTBUSTERS: THE VIDEO GAME—REMASTERED
■ If you like hunting spirits with Luigi, try this Ghostbusters tie-in. It looks and plays like a proper sequel—and even features the original stars.

PLUNGE AND PULL:
■ Fire a plunger at some objects and it will stick, with a short rope dangling. You can suck this in and slam the object to get it out of your way.

OVERWATCH 2

THE GREATEST HERO SHOOTER IS BACK WITH A TALE TO TELL

Overwatch has always had epic heroes with their own backstory, but when your game is a team-based shooter, it's not easy to tell a thrilling tale. That changes with Overwatch 2. The sequel pulls the Overwatch team back together and adds new co-op Story and Hero missions that bring you closer to the game's awesome stars. You don't have to imagine the next chapter in the Overwatch saga—you can play it through from the beginning to the end.

And on top of that? How about some new heroes, new maps, and even a new mode? The existing stars return with new looks and the odd tweak here and there, while Blizzard is promising even more great stuff to come. Everything we all loved about Overwatch is here, but now there's twice as much to love!

QUICK TIPS:

KNOW YOUR HEROES
■ Success in Overwatch 2 isn't just about knowing your hero's abilities, but about understanding all their strengths and weaknesses, and how they fit into a team. Keep playing with one or two heroes and make them your own.

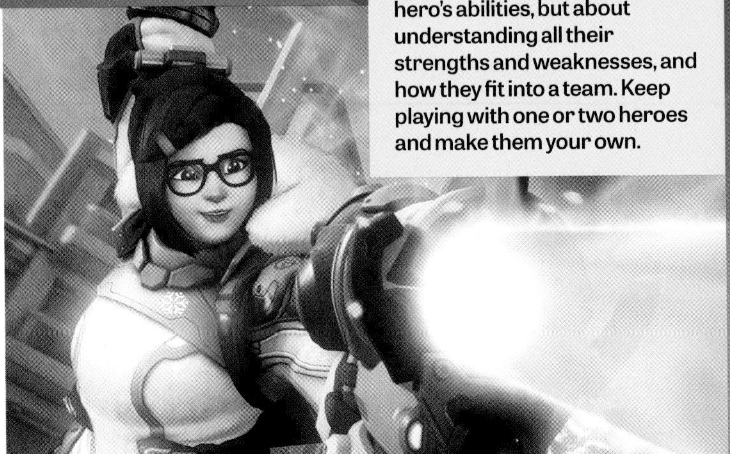

TAKE ONE FOR THE TEAM
■ Whether you're playing co-op or competitive, stop showboating and play for your teammates. Think about how you can use your abilities to support the other players.

FIND ANOTHER ROUTE
■ If enemies stand between you and your objectives, don't keep coming back for more. Look for another way to get past. You might even be able to get around and surprise them from behind!

BACK ON WATCH

■ In Overwatch 2, the Overwatch crew is back together in a battle against Null Sector: an army of artificially intelligent robots determined to put robot rights first at any cost.

FAST FACT:

Tracer isn't just one of Overwatch's most iconic heroes. She's the only survivor of Blizzard's Project Titan—a massive online sci-fi RPG that was cancelled before release.

■ You can't play through the whole campaign as your favorite hero—each player picks one of the four heroes in turn—but the missions build into an awesome Overwatch adventure.

■ Story missions are intense co-op missions where you take on one of four preset heroes, then fight through powerful Null Sector forces on the way to your next objective.

■ Hero missions put players on smaller, all-action missions, where they can take on more Null Sector robots or go into battle against the terrorist organization, Talon.

■ Through playing Hero missions, you can level up and customize your heroes. You can also supercharge their abilities, though this doesn't carry over into competitive games.

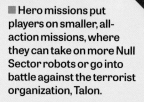

■ The Story and Hero missions also feature new co-op items, including healing stations that restore HP and corrosive grenades that boost the damage of all players' attacks.

ONE MORE PUSH

■ Push mode works like a big tug-of-war, where getting the block to the enemy base is a serious challenge. If neither team manages to get it there, the team that's pushed the block the farthest wins.

■ Overwatch 2 isn't just about the story stuff. It also has a brand-new multiplayer mode called Push. In Push, two teams compete to get a block to their opponent's base.

■ Try splitting the team so that, while some of you defend and guide the robot, others can interfere with the enemy team. Each Push map has useful side routes you can use to sneak around and attack from the sides or rear.

■ The only way to get it there is to persuade this robot to push the block in the right direction. With more of your team standing near the robot, he'll push the block your way, but if the other team controls him, he'll push it back toward your base.

NO ONE GETS LEFT BEHIND
■ One of the great things about Overwatch 2 is that it doesn't break up the original game's huge fan base. As long as you have Overwatch, you can still play in games with Overwatch 2 players, and use the same maps and heroes. You'll only miss out on all the new co-op story stuff.

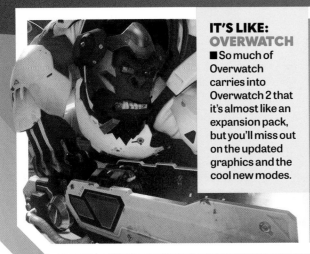

IT'S LIKE: OVERWATCH
■ So much of Overwatch carries into Overwatch 2 that it's almost like an expansion pack, but you'll miss out on the updated graphics and the cool new modes.

TRY: APEX LEGENDS
■ Apex takes the heroes and abilities of Overwatch and throws them into a Battle Royale. It can't match Overwatch 2 for variety, but it's a great game in its own right!

NEW HEROES, NEW LOOKS

■ All your Overwatch faves are back, even if they don't look exactly like they did before. Now the Overwatch crew is back together, most have had their outfits and gear updated.

■ With some, the differences are pretty subtle. Tracer gets new leggings, a new jacket, new goggles, fewer straps, and some box-fresh shoes.

■ Reinhardt, however, gets a new suit of armor with brighter yellow accents and a lion motif on his chest. He's also ditched his helmet, giving you a good look at his cool topknot and beard combo.

■ Echo is a familiar face to Overwatch fans—and a hero with some strong support abilities. As well as a gun that fires bombs she can detonate remotely, she has the power to copy her enemy's abilities and use them herself.

■ We also get some new heroes to play. Sojourn is another old member of the Overwatch, now back as a core part of the team. She comes packing a long-distance rifle and a high-powered blaster cannon.

CREATE
AND PLAY

Join the fun and create your own levels, games, and more

■ Games aren't just about playing anymore—they're becoming an outlet for your own creativity, giving you everything you need to build your own levels, worlds, movies, and many other amazing things. You don't need an expensive PC or software to do it, either. All the tools are provided within the game itself or available as a free download.

■ There's already a huge community of fans and budding game developers producing incredible stuff, and some of them are even making money or using it as a first step into a career in games. Want to join them? You can. All you need are the right games and your own great ideas.

Course Theme

300

Play

MEMORY USED
2,323 | 100,000

When you're ready to move on, go to **search** and choose a character from the **Quick Start Collection** to add to your **scene**.

rotate L2   ✕ / R2 stamp

0
100

GETTING CREATIVE

The tools we're talking about break down into three basic types:

■ Map Editors let you create maps, levels, or courses within your favorite games, using a selection of ready-made objects, scenery, characters, and items. You'll often be surprised how people can push different features to create very different or surprising worlds or game modes.

■ Other games have a range of built-in editing tools that enable you to create items or add-ons for the game, then share them with friends or other fans. For instance, a racing game might have a tool to make and customize cars, while a theme park management game might have one to create and share your own roller coasters.

■ Finally, some games work with separate add-on tools that you can download and use to make your own levels and characters, or even build whole games. These tend to be a bit more complex and difficult to learn, but are often much more powerful. You might even find that you're using the very same tools as the developers who made the original game!

SUPER MARIO MAKER 2 — Nintendo Switch

■ Super Mario Maker 2 is built around a clever and very easy-to-use level editor that you can use to make your own Mario levels. This isn't just a separate feature of the game, but a major part of it, so that you're learning how to use the tools as you play through it.

■ What's more, you can give the same level a range of different looks, so that it can resemble an old-school Super Mario Bros. level from 1985 or one from Super Mario 3D Land from 2013.

■ Fans have used Super Mario Maker 2 to make all kinds of unbelievable Mario levels. Some are incredibly difficult challenge levels, full of deadly traps and crazy jumps that demand split-second timing. Others work like clever machines, using different Mario game mechanisms to propel Mario from one end of the level to another without the player doing anything. Some of the ideas are so ingenious, they've even taught Nintendo a thing or two!

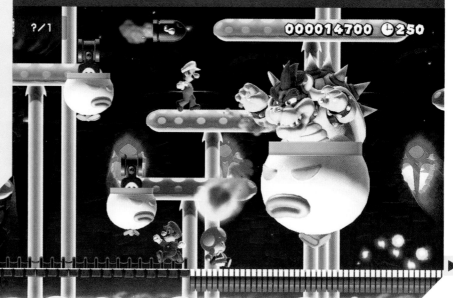

FROM DOOM TO DREAMS

■ We've had games with game-building tools for almost as long as we've had games. In 1983, we had programs like the Quill that you could use to write ancient text adventure games! Things really changed, though, with iD Software's classic first-person shooter, Doom. Within months of Doom's release, you could download level editors that enabled you to create your own Doom levels full of deadly demons to blast. Fans went wild, creating thousands of add-on levels, and even stringing them together into add-on games.

Counter-Strike and Defence of the Ancients, even became games in their own right. These tools were still complex and hard to use, so not everyone could get involved.

■ That's changed in the last 10 years or so. LittleBigPlanet (2008) was a platform game that included all the tools you needed to create your own platform games—and made it

all both easy and fun. Disney Infinity (2013) also had its own creative tools that you could use to build games around Disney and Pixar characters and their worlds.

■ Now dozens of games include their own map editors or course editors, while games like Fortnite, Roblox, and Dreams are taking game creation to a whole new level.

■ This spawned the whole "mod scene" that we still have today, where fans could use the editors and tools provided by a game's developers to make their own levels or modes. Some of these, like

ROBLOX PC, Xbox One

■ As you probably know, Roblox isn't a game itself, but a platform for creating and playing games. It includes its own game creation tool, Roblox Studio, which you can use to build your own worlds and fill them with objects, characters, and enemies, and even use the Lua programming language to create sophisticated games.

FORTNITE CREATIVE MODE

■ Fortnite Creative Mode has grown from a basic map editor for Fortnite into a sophisticated editor that you can use to build all sorts of games. It's actually one of the easiest tools to use, because you can just move a Fortnite character around and build using the regular Battle Royale building tools, or copy and paste bits of scenery from ready-made galleries that Epic Games provides.

SAVE THE WORLD

BATTLE ROYALE

CREATIVE
YOUR ISLANDS. YOUR FRIENDS. YOUR RULES.

◆ PLAY

SELECT A GAME MODE

■ You'll even find whole "prefab" buildings you can drop onto your map. There are new galleries with every Fortnite season, so you're never short of stuff to use.

■ Once you've built your little world, you can fill it with dozens of different devices, giving you traps, score counters, sensors to detect the player, and objects that spawn monsters when they get too close. You can also drop in chests full of weapons and gadgets, along with all the vehicles used in Fortnite's Battle Royale mode.

■ While there's no programming, you can combine different devices to control what happens when a player reaches a certain point or activates a switch, and the best map creators have used Creative Mode to produce some really amazing modes, maps, and mini-games. Epic shows the best of these off on its Featured Hubs, and some maps and modes even enter the main game as a Limited Time Mode.

■ Play Roblox and you'll find everything from racing games to RPGs to clones of Overwatch and Call of Duty. All of these were created using Roblox Studio!

■ Some of these games have hundreds of thousands of players. Roblox game makers can also make money from items or extras that gamers buy within the game. This has allowed some of them to turn their Roblox hobby into a business, making their own games or providing art or levels for other people's work.

MEET THE CREATOR:
WERTANDREW

Andreas Papoutsas, known in Fortnite as Wertandrew, is one of the most imaginative and best-known creators on the Fortnite Creative Mode scene.

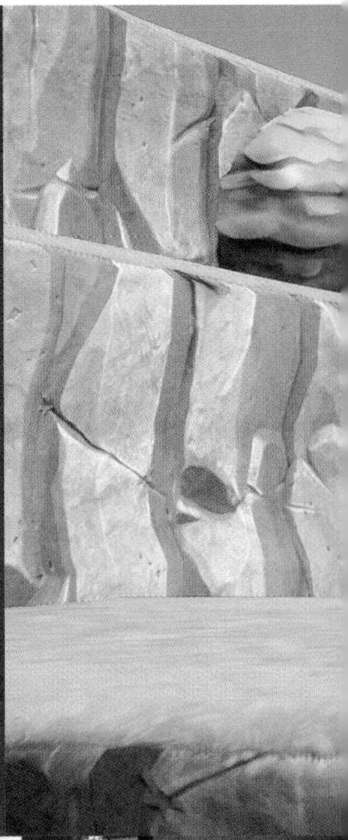

Q How easy does Fortnite make it to create your own games and levels?

A It's relatively easy. The grid helps you place construction pieces (the pieces that form the rooms in the game) with great ease, and the props are neatly categorized into various themes, so you can make anything you want. From a pirate town to a sci-fi spaceship, if you can think it you can build it. For me, I feel like I've been given all the LEGO pieces for free.

Another cool thing is that Fortnite is getting weekly updates and new things are being added all the time. Having all this for free, too, makes it a really good choice for people who want to try building and try their skill at level design.

🍄 **SUPER MANSU WORLD** 🍄
1597-9533-7823
CREATED BY: wertandrew 👥0/1
1-16 Players | Experience a grand journey featuring Mansu in his quest to save the princess! How far can you get? v1.1

🕐 3:51:32 👤

0
100

Q How much of creating a great map comes down to your imagination, and how much to your skill at using the different galleries and devices?

A It's more about imagination, I think. The skill will come on its own once you keep building, but imagination is something that comes from you. Of course, to really make something unique, you'll need both. But I feel that the most important thing is to have a "drive"; Something that will motivate you to keep going when things don't work the way you want them to, the level is getting too hard to test, or you can't find someone to test it.

Q What makes you proud when you produce a great map?

A Watching others play my maps in YouTube is my best reward. Seeing their live reaction while they play, to get frustrated or happy, to see what the problems with the map are (so I can fix them) is really enjoyable and makes my day. Sometimes I may watch the same video multiple times. Ha, ha! Getting featured is another, because more people try your map and you get a lot of feedback.

Q What's the best thing about making games in Fortnite?

A Fortnite has helped me grow a community and I now have millions of players who have tried my levels, which is something I never expected to achieve.

Thinking of it that way, this platform allows another player across the world to get free access to your game, play it, and feel happy. For the brief moment of time that they'll play your level, they'll forget their everyday problems and enjoy an experience that will entertain and help them feel better. That is something wonderful. The true achievement of Fortnite is that it helps to make a better, more enjoyable world for everyone.

DREAMS

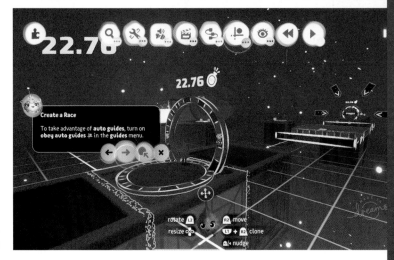

■ Dreams is the latest and greatest console game creation tool, giving PS4 gamers all they need to build games, graphics showcases, music videos, and more.

■ It comes from the same team as LittleBigPlanet, but where LittleBigPlanet was designed to build 2D platform games, Dreams can be used to make almost any style of game.

■ Already, we're seeing everything from 3D platform games in the style of Super Mario Odyssey to futuristic racing games, first-person shooters, retro arcade games, role-playing games, and puzzle games. There's almost nothing it can't do!

■ The way Dreams works is really clever, too. It has some brilliant tools for sculpting objects and landscapes out of 3D shapes and for creating your own characters and worlds. You can use other tools to make music or design levels with moving platforms, traps, enemies, obstacles, and items to collect.

■ Once you've published your game, other people can use all the bits you've created in their games, while you can use the things they've created in yours. Most people are better at one part of creating games than others, so if you're a natural artist, musician, or level designer, you can bring your dreams to life—and help other people with theirs!

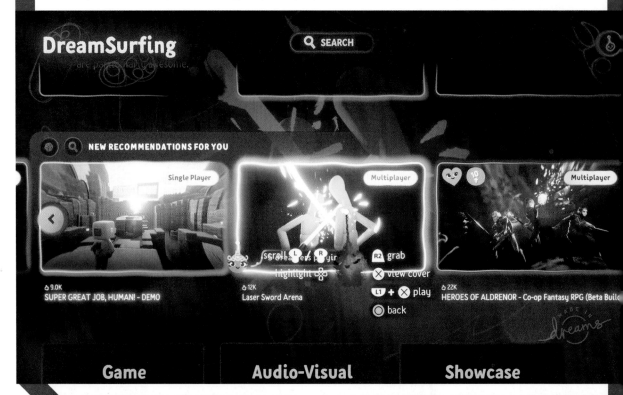

66

GET CREATIVE

■ Getting creative doesn't have to mean building games. Some games give you the creative tools to build other things that you can share.

■ For instance, Planet Coaster is a game that's all about building theme parks and filling them with the most amazing thrill rides. But it also gives you everything you need to make your own roller coasters, buildings, scenery, and whole themed areas, which you can share with the rest of the Planet Coaster community through the game.

■ Trials Rising is a brilliant 2D stunt-riding challenge game, where you try to ride your motorbike through some of the craziest courses you've ever seen. While it's packed with exciting levels, it also has its own in-game editor where you can craft your own, then share them with other Trials fans. If you love to make fiendish trials full of tricky obstacles and death-defying jumps, there are thousands of people out there who would love to try them!

MARVEL'S IRON MAN VR

Find out what it's like to wear the Iron Man suit. Have you ever dreamt of becoming one of Earth's mightiest heroes? With Marvel's Iron Man VR, you have your chance. The minute you clamp on your PlayStation VR helmet and pull down the visor, you can find yourself wearing the Iron Man suit, wielding Iron Man's weapons, and—best of all—flying like old shellhead himself. This is the nearest most of us will ever get to being a real superhero!

■ The team at Camouflaj has worked overtime to make flying and fighting as Iron Man feel natural and believable. When you're wearing the Iron Man helmet, you'll see the kind of heads-up display (HUD) that Tony Stark sees in the movies, and the whole game is played using a pair of PlayStation Move controllers.

■ The Move controllers act directly to control Stark's hands, and by holding them in different positions and at different angles, you have complete control over your movement and flight. Point your hands downward with the palms open, and Stark will speed into the air. Hold your hands parallel with your body with the palms downward, and he boosts forward at speeds of up to 200mph. Hope you don't get airsick!

■ It takes a bit of practice to get used to, but you'll soon find you can fly, boost, turn, and even hover using subtle movements of your body and hands. And the game doesn't hold you on to any rails, either. You can turn your head or body around and move in any direction, and fly wherever you want within the game's massive maps. Get ready for action around iconic locations, like Tony's California coast home and the Shield Helicarrier.

Captured from PS4 Pro

tured from PS4 Pro

■ Your hands are also crucial for firing and aiming the suit's weapons. Turn your palms off and aim outward, and you can fire off repulsor rays at hostile drones. Bring them in toward your chest, and you can blast the bad guys with your unibeam.

FAST FACT:

In the comics, this game's villain, Ghost, is usually a guy, but both here and in the movie *Ant-Man and the Wasp*, Ghost is female. She's a fierce match for the man of metal!

SEEN A GHOST?

■ Marvel's Iron Man VR gives us a new story based around a classic Iron Man villain, Ghost. You might remember a version of Ghost from the movie *Ant-Man and the Wasp*, where she's trying to steal Hank Pym's lab. In the game, though, she's driven by a rage against Tony Stark, wanting him to pay for his years as an arms manufacturer and the deaths his weapons have caused. Who is Ghost, and is this personal? You'll have to play the game to find out!

■ If your enemies get too close, charge toward them and give them your best shot. A quick punch should deflect most attackers, giving you a chance to blast them into shiny metal bits.

Captured from PS4 Pro

69

SPONGEBOB SQUAREPANTS:
BATTLE FOR BIKINI BOTTOM REHYDRATED

SPONGEBOB HAS NEVER LOOKED BETTER

I t's over 17 years since SpongeBob SquarePants: Battle for Bikini Bottom was released, but unlike most cartoon adaptations it hasn't been forgotten. That's partly because gamers just love SpongeBob. There's a reason why he's starred in three hit movies, and why we've been watching his antics on TV for over 20 years!

Battle for Bikini Bottom was a brilliant game. It got the fun and absurd humor of SpongeBob and his underwater posse, and it borrowed ideas from the best platform games of the era. And when that era includes games like Super Mario Sunshine, Jak and Daxter, and Ratchet & Clank, you know it was taking its ideas from the best!

But this isn't your usual "stick some HD textures on" remaster. The team at Purple Lamp Studios has redesigned all the graphics, tweaked and polished the gameplay, and even added a new two-player multiplayer mode!

FAST FACT:
The Robo Squidward boss battle appeared in the NDS version of Battle for Bikini Bottom, but never made it into the final console game. All we've ever seen before is concept art.

■ The game has had a complete visual upgrade, bringing all the characters, the scenery, the effects, and the lighting into the modern age. It's all running on the Unreal 4 engine—the same technology behind Fortnite, Star Wars Jedi: Fallen Order and a heap of other top games.

■ Hasn't SpongeBob changed? Check out the blocky edges, rough-looking textures, and flat lighting of the original PS2 game. Now take a look at the crisp, cartoon detail, shadows, and shiny black shoes of this year's remake.

BIG

PICTURE

■ This "Rehydrated" version doesn't just enhance the graphics. It also improves the gameplay, adding new features that weren't part of the original game. Some of the boss battles have been adjusted to make them less frustrating, while the Robo Squidward boss battle that was removed from the 2003 version finally makes its console debut. There's even a fun multiplayer mode, where you can team up with a friend to wipe the robot menace clean off Bikini Bottom.

■ It's not just SpongeBob who's had the upgrade treatment. All the old gang are back, and you can also play as Patrick or Sandy. Each has their own tasks to complete and their own unique skills.

SEA OF THIEVES

YO HO, YO HO, A PIRATE'S LIFE FOR ME

Sea of Thieves has transformed over the last few years, and whether you want a swaggering, swashbuckling adventure or timber-shivering sea combat, there's no better way to take to the waves. In January the game hit 10 million players, making it the most successful new Xbox game of the Xbox One era.

Set sail and it's not hard to see why. Sea of Thieves now has great tutorial missions to get your boots on deck, and once you're ready to pull up the anchor you can steer your way to some brilliant quests, including the Tall Tales that emerge from the briny depths with each new update. There are skeleton forts to be conquered, ships of the damned to be fought, mysterious chests to discover, and three different guilds to take on missions for. So strap on that cutlass and find yourself a scurvy crew; there are ships to sink and doubloons to be plundered!

QUICK TIPS:

HIT THE TAVERNS
■ Don't ignore the strange characters in taverns. Some, like Duke or Stitcher Jim, will have new Tall Tales and voyages you can go on—or can point you toward your next adventure.

CREATE A LEGEND
■ Umbra, who you'll find in the Lagoon of Whispers, is researching pirate legends and the deeds of the great buccaneers. Follow her clues and gather evidence, and there could be rare rewards.

BRITTLE BONES
■ All skeletons have their weakness. The shadow skeletons are vulnerable to light, gold skeletons hate water, while the mossy skeletons are weak against melee weapons.

HIGH ADVENTURE

TALL TALES
■ Tall Tales, like The Seabound Soul, put you on a quest that might involve ancient relics, battles with ghoulish pirates, and the freeing of trapped souls.

PETS
■ Every great pirate needs a pet, and each new update brings new cosmetics for them. Smarten them up for the holidays or give them a creepy look at Halloween.

SMOKE ON THE WATER
■ Firebombs can be fired out of cannons or thrown like grenades. Keep a bucket of water handy in case you need to stop the burning.

DEAD MAN'S CHEST
■ Ashen chests might contain rare loot or legendary tomes you can hand to Umbra to help her with her pirate legends. You'll need an Ashen key to open them, but they're well worth fighting over.

FAST FACT:
Firebombs have become one of the game's hottest accessories. Over 9 million of them were thrown in the first month they appeared, causing 1.5 million ships to be torched and over 600,000 pirates singed.

IT'S LIKE: DAUNTLESS
■ Looking for another big co-op adventure? Get a team together to hunt down monsters in this fantastic free-to-play hit.

TRY: PILLARS OF ETERNITY II: DEADFIRE
■ One of the best RPGs of recent years is a fantasy epic with an awesome pirate twist. And while it's brilliant on PC, PS4, and Xbox One, you can also play it on the move on Switch.

GO DYNAMAX!
POKÉMON SWORD & SHIELD

You might think of Pokémon as pint-sized creatures, but in the new Galar region they get much, much bigger. A Dynamaxed Pokémon is a giant-sized version, dishing out huge amounts of damage with supersized attacks.

■ You Dynamax a Pokémon using the special Dynamax band Professor Magnolia gives you early in the game. Dynamaxing a Pokémon will also increase its HP, though its other stats won't change. The health boost is based on the Dynamax Level, which you can increase by feeding your friend Dynamax Candy.

■ You'll also fight Dynamaxed Pokémon in Stadium Battles against Gym Leaders—they'll Dynamax their favorite critters—or in Link Battles against friends.

■ You can Dynamax in raid battles, where you'll fight wild Dynamaxed Pokémon. You'll need to go big to battle these bruisers and team up with friends or computer-controlled trainers.

FAST FACT:
Some Pokémon change shape when they're Dynamaxed, becoming amazing Gigantamax creatures.

■ You can only Dynamax a Pokémon for just three turns, and you can only Dynamax one Pokémon per battle. This means you need to time your Dynamaxing carefully and not waste it, or you could be stuck with a normal-sized Pokémon, getting stomped on by a big guy!

■ A Dynamaxed Pokémon swaps their usual moves for epic Max Moves. These have massive effects on the battlefield and are the most spectacular special moves in the game. Plus, when you're Dynamaxed, some attacks lose their secondary powers against you. Your Pokémon won't flinch or get swapped out in the middle of a turn!

DREAMS

Dreams isn't just another game—it's a way to create your own! Master Dreams' tools and you can build your own worlds, design your own characters, and turn your wildest ideas into games. You can create your own music and control how your world and its inhabitants behave. And you can put all this stuff together to make showcase scenes or short movies as well as fully playable games.

What's more, you don't have to do it alone. There's a big community of "Dreamers" already producing amazing stuff. You can surf the "Dreamverse" and try games of every type, from cute 3D platformers to racing games and arcade shoot 'em-ups. Like what you see? Why not remix it or borrow elements to create your own games? Or if you don't see yourself as a game designer, you can focus on level creation, character design, music, or animation, and help other Dreamers bring their dreams to life!

QUICK TIPS:

USE THE GRABCAM
■ Moving around in creative spaces can be slow, but move your Imp over an object and press R1 to lock on, and you can zoom directly to it using the left stick, or warp to it with L1.

SQUEEZE THE TRIGGERS
■ Moving and rotating objects can be tricky, but squeeze the triggers gently and you get slower but more accurate tools. Tapping the triangle button while moving or rotating can also help you get it right.

KEEP DREAMING
■ Before you get stuck into your own dreams, play a lot of other people's. You'll get more ideas about what's possible and you might find elements you can reuse.

EXPLORE THE DREAMVERSE

ART'S DREAM

■ In case players weren't sure what dreams they could make, the team behind Dreams created one of their own. Art's Dream tells the story of a jazz musician who has lost his way and left his band. Only by remembering his childhood dreams can he put his life back on the right track.

JAZZY NIGHTMARES

■ Art's Dream covers an amazing range of different game styles. One minute you're leaping from platform to platform in a fantasy world, the next you're searching for clues in a gloomy graphic adventure or playing a retro arcade shoot 'em up.

THE PILGRIM'S JOURNEY

■ The Dreams community is also building some cool stuff. The Pilgrim, by Dreamer Narvikgutten, is an incredibly polished platform adventure crammed with impressive scenery and some great gameplay ideas.

KURO'S ADVENTURE

■ Bawnanable's game, Kuro: A Shadow's Dream, is a polished 2D platform game with a ninja hero and some stunning Japanese landscapes. You've got to discover the power-ups in each level and use them to cross impossible gaps and reach new heights.

FAST FACT:

Dreams was one of the first games announced for PS4 back in 2013. It's taken over eight years for the team to get its game creation tools perfected!

EXPLORE LOST CITIES

■ And Dreams can do so much more than platform games. Dreamers are busy building first-person shooters, kart racing games, and their own Mario, Sonic, and Dragon Ball tributes. With some talent and a bit of practice, you can create incredible-looking worlds, like Chris_Redwalker 6's The Ancient Lost City.

DREAMS 101

Once Connie reaches the flag, head into Edit Mode again and go to the next step.

■ Media Molecule has done an incredible job with the tools you use to build your dreams, but putting stuff together in a 3D space isn't easy. Placing, moving, resizing, and rotating objects in your scenes takes some getting used to. Luckily, the game has some brilliant, fun tutorials to help with that.

■ The early ones feel almost like a puzzle game, where you're placing and moving blocks to help your conical hero reach a present. Later tutorials cover everything from building scenes to crafting characters, or adding colors and effects to your worlds. Each one gives you more rewards to play with. There's a lot to learn in Dreams, but Dreams makes learning fun!

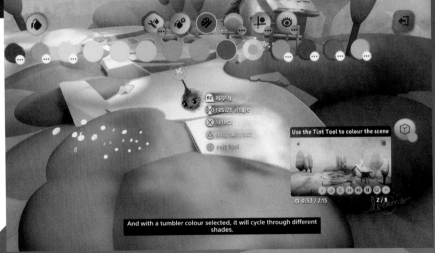

R2 apply
resize shape
select
add/subtract
exit tool

Use the Tint Tool to colour the scene

0:53 / 2.15   2 / 8

And with a tumbler colour selected, it will cycle through different shades.

IT'S LIKE: LITTLEBIGPLANET
■ LittleBigPlanet came from the same team as Dreams, and allowed you to both build and play brilliant 2D platform games—and more!

Place Sticker   Undo

TRY: FORTNITE CREATIVE MODE
■ Fortnite's Creative Mode isn't as powerful or as versatile as Dreams, but you can still use it to produce your own games and levels. Some have even become official Limited Time Modes.

DREAM YOUR OWN DREAMS

■ Play through a few games and run a few tutorials, and you'll be ready to start building your own dreams. This is where you really get to grips with Dreams' powerful editing tools.

■ You can use ready-made templates to get a head start, then add your own structures, characters, and cool contraptions. Don't worry if you're not artistic. You can either work with the objects and characters the Dreams team has created or reuse those built by others in the Dreams community.

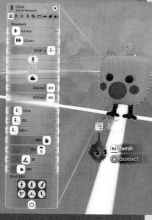

■ Nearly everything can be used and "remixed." Remix a character and you can change the way it moves or how it's animated, or even how far or how high it can jump.

resize shape

- R2 apply
- ✕ select
- △ add/subtract
- ◯ exit tool

■ Dreams also lets you program how your game world operates, just by dragging different blocks together into the world or into special control chips, then linking them together with wires. It works a lot like visual programming tools you might see in schools, like Scratch.

■ If you want to create your own original stuff, Dreams has the tools to help. You can build your own objects and characters from scratch, sculpting them from different 3D objects, and adding different colors, surfaces, and more.

ROBLOX

PLAY THE GAMES, THEN MAKE THE GAMES

Roblox goes from strength to strength, with nearly 10 million Roblox games and roughly 100 million players, making it one of the biggest gaming communities around. Whether you're playing on your PC, phone, or Xbox One, you can sign up, try some games, and have a great time. And if you've ever wanted to become a games artist or designer, you can download everything you need for free. It's not just a game, but a way to make, play, and share.

Roblox's biggest strength might be its variety. Bored of blasting zombies? Why not try delivering pizza, surviving a disaster, running a theme park, or joining a fantasy school? While you'll need a pocket full of Robux to play some games, a lot of them are free, meaning you can save your money for cool cosmetic items, extra levels, or in-game items. As soon as you're tired of one game, just hop on to the next. It's easy!

QUICK TIPS:

JUMP ON BOARD
■ You need to sign up and download some software for your PC, phone, or console before you can start playing, but once that's done you can play most games in a flash.

CHANGE THE SETTINGS OR QUIT
■ You can change the controls or settings on a game or leave it by accessing the Roblox Menu. Press the menu or options button on your controller or the Esc key on PC.

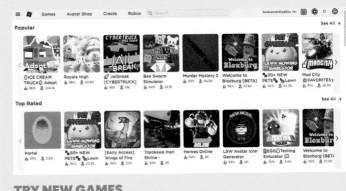

TRY NEW GAMES
■ Roblox lists all the current games in different categories, and you can check how popular a game is by seeing how many people have downloaded it—and how many of those have given it the thumbs-up.

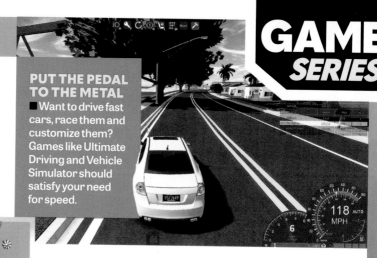

IN ROBLOX YOU CAN...

FIGHT ZOMBIES
■ Those Who Remain and Project Lazarus: Zombies give you all the zombie action you could want without the gore. Project Lazarus does a great impression of the classic Call of Duty Zombies mode.

PUT THE PEDAL TO THE METAL
■ Want to drive fast cars, race them and customize them? Games like Ultimate Driving and Vehicle Simulator should satisfy your need for speed.

GO TO SCHOOL
■ For something with a gentler pace, try Royale High. It's a high school fantasy role-playing game where princes and princesses go to classes, meet magical creatures, and take on mini-games.

JOIN THE BATTLE ROYALE
■ If you have a favorite game, there's probably a Roblox clone out there. Island Royale is basically Fortnite, while Q-Clash looks and plays a lot like Overwatch.

BUILD A THEME PARK
■ If you'd like to fill a park with rides and roller coasters, give Theme Park Tycoon 2 or Water Park World a spin. You can even see your fellow Robloxians enjoy it!

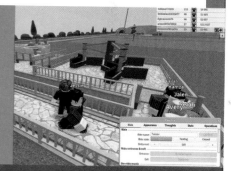

FAST FACT:
Want to learn about games development? Roblox could be a great way in. The makers even partnered with Star Wars in 2019 to create an educational Galactic Speedway creator challenge for kids.

IT'S LIKE: MINECRAFT
■ Roblox shares Minecraft's creativity and easy-to-pick-up gameplay, though it goes even further in allowing you to build your own games.

TRY: FORTNITE
■ Fortnite's best known for its Battle Royale mode, but its Creative Mode has powerful tools for creating your own worlds, levels, and single-player and multiplayer games.

APEX LEGENDS

PROVE THAT YOU'RE A LEGEND

Fortnite has the fun factor, and we all know that PUBG came first, but if you're after the best battle royale game Apex Legends is a serious contender. Now well into its second year, it's faster-paced and more intense than the competition, with the best run-and-gun gameplay in the business. We also love the lineup of legends, which rival Overwatch's crew for cool.

In its first season, Apex was at risk of becoming boring, but the team at Respawn has fixed that with sweeping changes for each big update. Apex now has two maps to work with, which themselves have seen big transformations, while new legends have introduced new styles of play and strategies to try. Apex is tougher and more demanding than Fortnite—and its grittier sci-fi approach isn't for everyone—but it's every bit as exciting. Can you resist just one more drop?

QUICK TIPS:

STICK TOGETHER
■ Play well with your teammates, ping them weapon and enemy locations and revive them, and you've got a better chance of surviving. Go lone wolf and you just won't last.

LEARN THE LEGENDS
■ Find a legend or two who really suit your play style, and get to grips with their abilities. It's these that make a difference between a top-five finish and an early exit.

PLAY SNEAKY
■ While some legends work into straight offensive play styles, others reward sneaky behavior. Learn how to use Caustic's gas traps, or bamboozle the enemy with Mirage's decoys.

MOVE IT!

■ Apex has changed a lot since Season 1. For a start, we now have two maps to contend with: the original King's Canyon and the wintery World's Edge.

■ Only one map is in play at any time, and the game can switch between them in the middle of a season, as it did in Season 4.

■ As in every battle royale, the biggest threat isn't always another team—it could be the ring closing in on you, draining your health and shields in seconds!

FAST FACT:

Apex Legends shares its universe and some of its visual style with Respawn's excellent Titanfall games. Evil corporations like Hammond Robotics and the IMC exist in both games, and some of the weapons carry over.

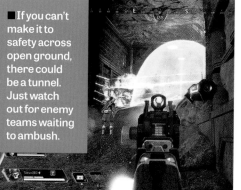

■ If you can't make it to safety across open ground, there could be a tunnel. Just watch out for enemy teams waiting to ambush.

■ While Apex doesn't do vehicles, there are ways to get to safety faster. You can use the zip lines and slide down slopes at speed, or take a fast rope up to the red balloons (or jump towers) and relaunch yourself toward the ring.

■ The World's Edge map even has a train you can catch—or land on if you're dropping in. It's well supplied with loot and weapons, and you can hop off whenever you like. After all, who's going to ask Caustic or Revenant for their ticket?

IT'S LIKE: FORTNITE BATTLE ROYALE

■ Apex Legends' biggest battle royale rival is still a massive game and, like Apex, it never stops changing. It's easy to get into, never boring and as much fun as any shooter out there.

TRY:
THE CYCLE

■ Looking for a different style of sci-fi shooter? The Cycle mixes co-op and competitive play, so that you're fighting both with and against other players to complete exciting missions. Underrated.

ESPORTS

THE BIGGEST GAMES, THE GREATEST PLAYERS

So, you want to be an eSports pro? You're going to have to work hard and train even harder, developing the high-level skills required to win at the world's biggest games. Want to know what it takes to be a champion? Read on and find out!

FORTNITE BATTLE ROYALE

■ Fortnite took the basic idea of the battle royale—100 players land on an island and scavenge for weapons, and only one player leaves alive—and added its own spin. Players can build their own walls, ramps, towers, and other structures, and use them for protection or to overpower the competition.

■ Sharp reflexes and shooting skills will only get you so far. Winning that Victory Royale takes strategy and knowledge of the different traps and weapons. Most of all, you need to master the build controls, so that you don't get beaten in "build battles".

MAIN EVENT

FORTNITE WORLD CUP

■ Several seasons of Solo and Duos tournaments ending with a massive three-day Finals competition. In 2019, over two million viewers watched 17-year-old Bugha win the $3 million cash prize.

OVERWATCH/ OVERWATCH 2

■ Blizzard's brilliant first-person shooter takes the stale gameplay of the old "team deathmatch" games and gives it a bigger, brighter personality. Borrowing a few ideas from games like DOTA2 and League of Legends, it serves up fast-paced battles between teams of heroes, each with their own look, and signature abilities and attacks.

■ Lightning reflexes and awesome aim are crucial, but the real trick to mastering Overwatch is understanding what makes each hero special— and how you can use their abilities to counter other heroes and support your team.

OVERWATCH WORLD CUP

■ The world's best players are voted onto national teams, which then compete at the annual BlizzCon conference.

MAIN EVENT

DOTA2

■ Defence of the Ancients 2 is the sequel to one of the first Multiplayer Online Battle Arena (MOBA) games—and one of the biggest eSports in the world. Players pick a champion and help their team wage war on the other team, aiming to destroy their heavily defended base.

■ Mop up the computer-controlled "creeps," and you earn gold you can spend on new abilities. You need these to crush the other team's heroes on the battlefield.

■ Like any MOBA game, DOTA2 is all about quick thinking, teamwork, and tactics. The map is built around three lanes that connect the two bases, and you need to make sure that each lane is properly defended while pushing hard where the enemy looks weak.

MAIN EVENT

THE INTERNATIONAL

■ An epic tournament that sees 18 teams compete for a $34 million prize pool. 2019's ninth International tournament was watched by over 1.97 million viewers.

LEAGUE OF LEGENDS

■ League of Legends launched after DOTA, but it's now the number one MOBA for players and viewers. Players can pick from a roster of around 150 champions, then take them out into the Fields of Justice to battle the other team. Kill minions, monsters, and enemy champs, and you can equip your champion with new gear.

■ Like DOTA2, League of Legends is all about fast reactions, tactics, and teamwork. It's a bit easier to start with than its rival, but you really need to know your champions to push ahead.

MAIN EVENT

LEAGUE OF LEGENDS WORLD CHAMPIONSHIP

■ Twenty-four teams rise through regional tournaments to make it to the final and a chance for a slice of the $2.2 million prize fund. The 2019 final was the most watched eSports event of 2019.

HEARTHSTONE

■ Blizzard's collectible card game borrows troops, heroes, and villains from its Warcraft titles for one-on-one battles where players take turns to play cards from their deck. You can use abilities, cast spells, or summon minions to attack. By winning matches and completing quests you earn gold to buy new cards.

■ Hearthstone is a massive hit, with more than 100 million players across PCs, consoles, smartphones and tablets. Its fast pace and sneaky strategies have also made it a popular eSport, with millions of loyal fans on Twitch.

MAIN EVENT

HEARTHSTONE WORLD CHAMPIONSHIP

■ The world's top players face off in a series of tournament matches. In the 2019 championship, the winner, HunterAce, won $250,000 in a final watched by over a quarter of a million viewers.

ROCKET LEAGUE CHAMPIONSHIP SERIES

■ The Rocket League Championship Series has qualifying rounds around the globe, finishing in a 12-team playoff and a gripping championship final. NRG eSports won the 2019 Season 8 tournament plus a huge $200,000 first prize.

ROCKET LEAGUE

■ Just about everyone loves Rocket League—the game where rocket-powered vehicles play soccer, working as a team to smash the ball into the opposing team's goal. Skillful players ram the other team's cars to destruction, or fire themselves into the air to knock the ball across the field.

■ It's no surprise that Rocket League has become a massive eSport, with its own leagues, events, and Championship Series. The game is easy to get into, tough to master and a lot of fun while you're learning.

MAIN EVENT

THE TOP ESPORTS PLAYERS

KYLE "BUGHA" GIERSDORF

■ Bugha came out of nowhere to clinch the 2019 Fortnite World Cup, establishing himself as one of the fastest, fiercest players in the game. Even though he's only 17 years old, talent, training and sheer hard work have made him the Fortnite star to beat.

JOHAN "NOTAIL" SUNDSTEIN

■ The Danish DOTA2 superstar has helped his team, OG, to two International tournament victories and earned nearly $7 million. In 2019, he became the most successful eSports champion ever.

LEE "FAKER" SANG-HYEOK

■ A true eSports legend, Faker is one of only two players to have won the League of Legends World Championship three times. He was defeated in the 2019 semi-finals, but he's still notching up international wins. Expect a comeback.

PARK "PROFIT" JOON-YEONG

■ Originally a star player for the championship-winning London Spitfire team, Profit is one of the fastest, most aggressive players on the Overwatch scene. Now signed to Seoul Dynasty, he's a master of the game's high-damage heroes.

THE NEW LEGENDS

Like any great online action game, Apex Legends won't stand still—it's always adding new maps, new weapons, and new legends. With every new season comes a new contender, bringing a new style and different tactics to the battle.

WATTSON

■ Natalie "Wattson" Pacquette helped design the Apex Games arena, but that didn't keep her from jumping inside it and fighting the world's best (and worst). She's a great defensive fighter if you can keep her stocked up with Ultimate Accelerants and use her abilities, but don't get stuck to the spot. In Apex, you need to keep moving!

SPARK OF GENIUS

■ One Ultimate Accelerant will fully charge Wattson's Ultimate, while standing near an Interception Pylon will reduce her tactical ability cooldown times.

PERIMETER SECURITY

■ Place one node after another to create an electric fence to block an opening or surround a small area. Enemies trying to pass through will have their movement slowed and take a nasty dose of damage.

INTERCEPTION PYLON

■ Wattson's Ultimate creates a compact electrified pylon that destroys some incoming projectiles, including grenades and Gibraltar's and Bangalore's special attacks. It also gives friendly shields a boost.

CRYPTO

■ This genius hacker lives to break through security and uncover the secrets of the galaxy's biggest corporations. Nobody knows his real name, his age or his history, or even why he wants justice or revenge. One thing's for sure, though: Crypto is a brilliant support character for anticipating battles and gaining the advantage before you join a fight.

SURVEILLANCE DRONE

■ Crypto can use his drone companion to get a sneaky peek at the surrounding area and pick out enemies, weapons, ammo, loot and more. It's speedy with impressive range, but weak. If it's shot down, you'll have to wait 40 seconds for another drone.

NEUROLINK

■ The technology embedded in Crypto's brain keeps him linked to his drone at all times. Enemies detected within 30 meters of your position will be marked out—and your teammates will see them, too.

DRONE EMP

■ Charge up your Ultimate and you can trigger an EMP shockwave from the drone. It will damage shields, disable traps, and slow down your enemies. Get in and hit them hard while they're off balance!

FAST FACT:

Respawn teased players with a different Season 4 champion, Forge, only to have Revenant murder him and steal his spot.

REVENANT

■ He used to be a human assassin, but Revenant lost his humanity long ago at the hands of a criminal empire, becoming an android angel of death. Now the only emotion he feels is the desire for revenge. He's equipped to get it, too, with abilities that make him a tough target in close-quarters battles!

STALKER

■ Revenant crouch-walks faster and jumps higher than other legends, making him extra-sneaky and hard to pin down.

SILENCE

■ Revenant's device deals damage and disables enemy abilities. Toss it at an enemy team, then get them while they're weak.

DEATH TOTEM

■ Revenant's Ultimate creates a totem that, when used by friend or foe, will return them to it if they're killed or downed.

FORTNITE CHAPTER 2

THE SECOND CHAPTER IS EVEN BETTER THAN THE FIRST!

Fortnite isn't going anywhere. Epic Games' Battle Royale mega-hit has come out of its glorious first chapter into a second that's crammed brilliant ideas. We've already had an all-new map, new game modes, more movie and music crossovers, and a crazy spy-themed makeover, with bosses, mythic weapons, henchmen, and disguises. You never know where Fortnite's going next!

While Battle Royale is still the heart and soul of Fortnite, it's growing as a game as well. Creative Mode has given the community all the tools it needs to create great maps and modes, and the community returned the favor with all types of weird and wonderful stuff. Meanwhile, Fortnite's Save the World co-op mode also keeps getting better, with some superb seasonal events all of its own.

Fortnite faces some strong rivals in Apex Legends and Call of Duty's Warzone mode, but nothing else gives you so much fun with each new season or such a strong package. And while it's tempting to spend a fortune on new outfits and other cosmetics, you can still play Fortnite free of charge.

THE SECOND CHAPTER

A NEW MAP

■ Chapter 2 launched with a brand-new map and all-new landing spots and points of interest. Fortnite being Fortnite, though, it's changing more with every new season.

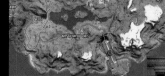

RB PLACE MARKER   LB REMOVE MARKER

NEW VEHICLES

■ From karts to planes to the mighty Baller, Chapter 1 gave players some great vehicles to speed around in. With its motorboats and the flying, fighting Choppa, Chapter 2 is dishing out even more goodies.

BOTS TO BATTLE

■ You're not just up against human enemies anymore. Computer-controlled foes give less skilled players a fighting chance to get better, while Season 2 gave us the Henchmen bots for cool spy movie action.

FAST FACT:

40 million players competed to qualify for a space in the 2019 Fortnite World Cup finals, and the average age of finalists was just 16.

QUICK TIPS:

LEARN YOUR LANDING SPOTS

■ To get the best guns and gadgets in the early-game, you need to know where to land and where to look for chests. Pick a favorite landing spot and learn it inside out.

GET BUILDING

■ Building makes the difference between victory and defeat. Learn to build and you can move faster, protect yourself and get a huge advantage when fighting. Practice every chance you get.

READY TO RUMBLE

■ If you're out of practice, play the Team Rumble mode. You'll get plenty of combat and some building in bite-sized games where you can respawn if you die.

CUSTOM OUTFITS

■ We're used to being able to pick different skins or outfits and customize them with pickaxes, back bling, and gliders. Chapter 2 has taken this to a whole new level with outfits where you can change the hair, the clothes, and even the face.

SAVE THE WORLD

■ Save the World is Fortnite's co-op game mode, where teams of four players work together to battle evil zombie Husks and their Mist Monster friends. It has an epic campaign that takes in different types of mission, where you could be defending your homebase against a Husk onslaught, rescuing survivors or attacking Husk encampments.

■ Save the World used to be hard to get into, over-complicated and maybe just a little bit dull, but Epic has got rid of the most boring stuff and made the game easier to learn. There's now a real thrill in working together to defeat a horde of Husks, and Save the World has its own fun personality.

IT'S LIKE: PLAYERUNKNOWN'S BATTLEGROUNDS

■ PUBG was the first Battle Royale to hit it big, but it's nowhere near as colorful or fun-loving as the reigning champ.

TRY: APEX LEGENDS
■ Apex Legends is the best of Fortnite's rivals, giving you a gritty, sci-fi take on Battle Royale with a hint of Overwatch in its legendary heroes.

CHAPTER 2'S TOP LANDING SPOTS

STEAMY STACKS

■ Sitting in the northeast corner of the map, it's hard to miss this industrial complex with its massive chimneys. There are always chests on the rooftops and even more lurking in the many rooms, and you can get launched into the air from the two stacks for a quick glide out toward the storm circle.

SLURPY SWAMP

■ While it wouldn't be a great place to live, the swamp is a good place to land. All those mushrooms, tankers and barrels of blue goo can top up your shields and you'll still find some guns worth having. You might have to run for the storm circle if it's over the other side of the map!

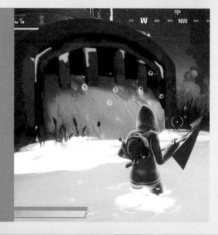

RETAIL ROW

■ One of the few classic locations to survive the move to Chapter 2, though the shops and the layout have changed. The supermarket, shops, and restaurants are great for stocking up with guns and shields. Just watch out for snipers!

DIRTY DOCKS

■ Maybe the name puts players off, but this west coast location is often quiet and stacked with loot. Have a good look around, find the chests, then grab a boat and make your escape. There should be some chests out of easy reach up on the cranes and the pylon on the hill.

WHAT MAKES FORTNITE SPECIAL?

"Fortnite's stayed so popular because it never stands still. There are always new weapons, new modes, or new venues to explore in Battle Royale. And when something doesn't work, it's banished from the game quickly!"

Barry Collins, Editor, Independent and Unofficial Guide to Fortnite magazine

FRENZY FARMS

■ If you're looking for a more central landing spot, give Frenzy Farms a try. There's a massive farmhouse and several barns and silos to explore, along with some crop fields where you can creep up on unsuspecting players. You can also make a quick escape to Pleasant Park, Salty Springs, or the old Agency island.

OVERWATCH SIGMA AND ECHO

Sigma and Echo are two of Overwatch's most challenging characters. Who are they, and how should you play them?

SIGMA

Dr. Siebren de Kuiper was a brilliant astrophysicist, famous for his research into gravity. While developing his theories, he conducted a daring experiment on the International Space Station.

The experiment went wrong, triggering a tiny anomaly in space-time, which affected the doctor both mentally and physically. Gravity behaved differently around him, while he became obsessed with the hidden nature of the universe at the expense of his own humanity.

Kuiper was locked away to prevent him becoming a danger to the human race, but the terrorist group, Talon, infiltrated the facility and broke him out so he could work on their behalf. Using his codename, Sigma, he wields awesome gravitational abilities—and he's not going to use them for the good of mankind.

SIGMA ABILITIES

Hyperspheres: Primary attack. Sigma fires two rounds of projectiles that explode on impact, damaging multiple enemies at once. The projectiles can also bounce around corners to hit unseen foes.

Experimental Barrier: Sigma can send a floating barrier to any position in his view, and bring it back at any time.

Kinetic Grasp: Sigma stops and holds incoming projectiles in mid-air, transforming them into protective shields.

Accretion: Sigma can drag a mass of debris from the battlefield and send it flying at the enemy of his choice.

Gravitic Flux Ultimate: Sigma switches gravity to send enemies flying into the air, then reverses the effect to slam them down to the ground with a thud.

SIGMA TIPS

■ Practice using Sigma's Hyperspheres. They do a lot of damage, but the range is hard to judge. Learn to predict where they'll bounce and explode, and you'll really hit the enemy hard.

■ Keep using Experimental Barrier to protect yourself and the team, recalling it every now and then to fire off some Hyperspheres and recharge the shield.

■ Use Accretion to knock down enemies and stop them unleashing their ultimate moves.

ECHO

Echo is a robot designed by Dr. Mina Liao. Liao was an expert in robotics and AI, and was involved in creating the military robots that attacked humanity in the Omnic Crisis. After the crisis, she was recruited by Jack Morrison, becoming one of the earliest members of the Overwatch team.

At Overwatch, Liao worked on the computer system, Athena, while also trying to build Echo, a revolutionary adaptive robot designed to help Overwatch handle future world problems. Sadly, Liao was killed by a mysterious enemy force, but not before completing her final project.

Echo was built to learn from and mimic other's abilities and behavior, and after spending hours observing her creator, she's become an echo of the scientist. Reluctant to risk using Echo after Liao's death, Overwatch stopped all development and put her in quarantine, but with the world once again in peril she has been let loose!

FAST FACT:

Echo was actually one of the first characters designed for Overwatch, based on concept art for Blizzard's unfinished game, Project Titan. She was the final hero to be added in Overwatch before the launch of Overwatch 2.

ECHO ABILITIES

Tri-Shot: Primary attack. Three shots fired at once in a triangle pattern.

Sticky Bombs: Secondary attack. A volley of sticky explosives that detonate after a short delay.

Focusing Beam: Echo fires a narrow beam of high-damage energy that does additional damage to enemies on low health.

Flight and Glide: Echo can take flight with a quick burst of speed, and glide down to Earth when she's falling.

Duplicate: Ultimate ability. Echo can scan the targeted enemy and copy their abilities.

ECHO TIPS

■ Echo's Duplicate Ultimate is incredibly powerful, not just because you can copy your enemy's abilities, but because their Ultimate will charge up faster.

■ Focusing Beam is a great finishing move or very useful in confined areas, where your enemy's movement is restricted.

■ Practice Echo's Flight and Glide moves. You get a sudden burst of speed, followed by a few seconds where you have more control, before the final glide down to the ground.

SPELLBREAK

SWAP BULLETS FOR SORCERY IN A MAGICAL BATTLE ROYALE

Spellbreak isn't trying to be Apex Legends or Fortnite—it's a spell-slinging fantasy take on the Battle Royale. Here, you fight as a powerful battlemage, confronting rival wizards in the ruins of the Hollow Lands. Instead of guns, you wear enchanted gauntlets, allowing you to harness all the powers of fire, stone, ice, and wind. Can you level up and destroy your opponents, or will you fall victim to the fury of the spellstorm?

Okay, so it sticks to the Battle Royale rules, but when you play it has a different feel. Your sorcerers are much more mobile, using flight and teleportation to move around the map. They can combine their elemental powers in different ways, allowing you to boost or counter an attack. Don't get stuck in muggle mode—give this wizard Battle Royale a try!

QUICK TIPS:

KEEP MOVING
■ This isn't the kind of game where you can sneak around until the final ten. You've got to get in there, dodge and evade attacks, and use your skills and spells to hit back harder.

FIND THE SHRINES
■ The areas marked with yellow rings are shrines, where you can grab free skill points and easy loot.

WATCH YOUR MANA
■ Mana is the magical energy you need to use your magic powers and cast your spells. Run out and you're almost defenseless, so either wait for your mana to regenerate or find a mana potion.

A GAME OF GAUNTLETS

■ Forget guns. In Spellbreak, it's all about the gauntlets. There are six different types, and you wear two at a time, each one giving you one fast main attack and one more powerful secondary attack.

■ The stone gauntlets slam down on the ground for a deadly shockwave, while the venom gauntlets fire poison missiles that leave a deadly pool on the ground. The lightning gauntlets blast the enemy with lightning bolts.

■ The fire gauntlets throw fireballs, while the ice gauntlets shoot an icy missile, accompanied by a trail of ice along the ground. You can even slide along it for some extra speed!

■ The secondary attacks do more damage. Call in a lightning storm or wall of fire, or hurl a massive boulder at your foes.

IT'S LIKE: FORTNITE
■ Fortnite keeps setting the standards for other Battle Royale games to follow—and it has a magic of its own!

■ As well as your gauntlets, you can carry magical runes, which give you the power of flight, invisibility, or teleportation. They work for a short while, but then need a quick pause to recharge.

TRY: MAGES OF MYSTRALIA
■ Looking for a game with an ingenious magic system? This indie hit action RPG allows you to design your own spells. Whatever the monster or problem, you can cast your way around it.

FAST FACT:
There's more to Spellbreak than just the Battle Royale. The devs are talking about more modes, including more team modes and even a co-op campaign, where mages could join forces against an evil foe.

■ Each player also picks two classes, which you can switch between during a match. Each class has its own bonus perks for different abilities, and you can power these up by earning skill points as you fight.

MEET GOOIGI!
LUIGI'S MANSION 3

Even the toughest hero can't clear a haunted hotel on their own—and Luigi isn't tough. In fact, he's as cowardly as they come. Luckily, Professor E. Gadd has invented the ultimate ghost-hunting companion: a living, moving goo that becomes Luigi's clone.

■ Gooigi's biggest strength is that he can push through obstacles Luigi can't get through. As his Jello-like body can squeeze through bars or shutters or into narrow holes, you can use Gooigi to enter closed-off rooms, grab objects and even suck up nearby ghosts.

■ Once your Poltergust is filled with Gadd's green goo, you can summon Gooigi with a click of the right stick. You can switch control from Gooigi to Luigi and back again, or put the gooey guy back in storage with a double-click.

■ Gooigi has his own goo flashlight and Poltergust cleaner, so he can use the same flash, suck, and slam moves as the real-deal Luigi. He doesn't have as much health as Luigi, though, so you might not want to use him for the more difficult battles. Still, you can always spawn a new Gooigi when one goes down.

■ You can also pair Luigi and Gooigi by switching between them. Set Luigi to work, say, blowing on a crucial fan mechanism, and you can switch to Gooigi, point his Poltergust at the same thing, and the two will blow on it together for double the air power. It's a skill you'll need to solve puzzles—and even to beat some ghosts!

■ Luigi and Gooigi can also work for two or more players. If you're playing the main adventure, a second player can take control of Gooigi so you don't have to switch. You can also play as different colors of Gooigi in the ScreamPark and ScareScraper multiplayer modes.

FAST FACT:

Gooigi made his first appearance in Luigi's Mansion 2: Dark Moon, where he represented a second player in the multiplayer mode. He also turns up in Super Smash Bros. Ultimate for some of Luigi's special attacks.

GOOIGI MULTIPLAYER
■ Gooigi has one fatal weakness: Water breaks down his green goo! Avoid any puddles or sprays of water when you're playing Gooigi, or your slime-stuffed clone will dissolve!

PSYCHONAUTS 2

A TRIP INSIDE A DERANGED DENTIST'S MIND

Things are crazy in the world of Psychonauts 2, where our hero, Raz, has joined the ranks of the Psychonauts: psychic superspies who can infiltrate the twisted minds of notorious villains. The 2005 original is a real cult classic, and this new sequel has been in development for a whole five years.

Psychonauts reveled in its bizarre worlds and puzzle-platformer gameplay, and this sequel is no different. This first level takes us inside the bonkers brain of Dr. Caligosto Loboto, the diabolical dentist from the first game, as Raz goes undercover to discover the evil genius behind a new threat. It's a rocking reintroduction to this oddball universe, and a chance to come to grips with Raz's powerful psychic skills.

FAST FACT:
Raz is the short name of Razputin Aquato, the young psychic who—in the first game—defies his family to become a Psychonaut. Raz is now a full member of the team, and the boyfriend of its leader's daughter, Lili.

■ Psychonauts 2 is—at heart—a 3D platformer, but you won't find worlds as weird as these in your average Super Mario game. It's also packed with puzzles. You'll have to use brains as well as brawn to fight your way through these mangled minds.

■ The level starts with a day in a dull, boring office, but soon descends into a nightmare of endless gums and shining teeth. You'll be hounded by savage dentures and rubber-stamping censors determined to stamp you out!

■ As in the first game, Raz wields a range of psychic powers, setting objects on fire, moving objects with his mind, and rolling around at high speeds on a levitating ball of thought. These aren't his only powers, though, and you can expect more later on in the game.

TOP 10

THESE GAMING STARS PACK SOME AWESOME ABILITIES

HERO POWERS

1

MIRAGE FROM APEX LEGENDS
PSYCHE OUT AND VANISHING ACT

■ Mirage causes chaos on the battlefield, combining cloaking abilities with fast-moving decoys. With Psyche Out, they'll shoot at a single decoy and reveal their location. With Vanishing Act, Mirage disappears while a group of decoys spawn around him. Good luck tracking down the real Mirage.

2

ROAD HOG FROM OVERWATCH
CHAIN HOOK

■ It doesn't sound like much, but the Hog's hook has so many uses. It will not just damage your foes but tug them helplessly toward you, so you can finish them off with a blast of your scrap gun. Or why not hook an enemy hero while they're trying to use an ability, stopping them dead in their tracks?

3

WARLOCK STORMCALLER FROM DESTINY 2: FORSAKEN
CHAOS REACH

■ We love the Supers in Destiny 2. It's tough going toe-to-toe with space monsters, but charge up your Super and it's payback time! Take the Warlock Stormcaller's Chaos Reach. This massive beam of storm energy shines a mighty light on the toughest enemy.

4

WRAITH FROM APEX LEGENDS
INTO THE VOID AND DIMENSIONAL RIFT

■ Need to escape or get through an enemy? Nothing beats turning invisible and speeding past them. However, Wraith's portal-making powers are even stronger. With your help, your team can cross canyons at high speed, get straight through a wall, or turn the tables on enemies setting up an ambush.

5

6

REAPER FROM OVERWATCH
DEATH BLOSSOM
■ Other Overwatch heroes (or villains) can do more damage, but Reaper's shotgun-based attacks make him deadly at close range, and his Death Blossom ultimate is one of the most spectacular abilities in the game. It will wipe out every enemy around!

CAUSTIC FROM APEX LEGENDS
NOX GAS TRAP AND NOX GAS GRENADE
■ Some people love a sneaky hero with a talent for traps, and Caustic is one of the best. His Nox Gas Traps are ideal for poisoning enemies, and you can drop six before they start disappearing. His Ultimate puts the same stuff in a grenade for throwing.

7

8

BAPTISTE FROM OVERWATCH
IMMORTALITY FIELD
■ Baptiste is one of gaming's greatest support characters, thanks to a range of super healing and protection powers. You've got a gun that can heal as well as hurt, plus a healing burst that heals all teammates around you. Immortality Field is best, though. While your allies are in its zone, they just won't die. How's that for taking care of the team?

GROVER FROM PALADINS
WHIRLWIND
■ Is he Groot? If not, he must be a close cousin. The giant walking tree has some amazing abilities to trap and heal, plus a vine grapple move. His best move, though, is his Ultimate: Whirlwind. Charge it up, spin around, and transform into a typhoon of destruction.

9

10

HUNTER GUNSLINGER FROM DESTINY 2: FORSAKEN BLADE BARRAGE
■ Here's another top Destiny 2 Super: Blade Barrage. Fill your Supers meter and you can leap into the air, pause for a second, and fling flaming golden blades in all directions. Best of all, the things explode! Sorry, bad guys, here comes the sun!

DROGOZ FROM PALADINS
DRAGON PUNCH
■ Drogoz is a winged lizard with a rocket launcher in a world of sword-wielding fantasy dudes. His secondary attack involves venomous, burning spit. Best of all, his Dragon Punch is a flying haymaker that's guaranteed to be a knockout blow.

DIGIMON SURVIVE

A NEW STYLE OF DIGIMON ADVENTURE

Everything's changing for Digimon in Digimon Survive, the latest in the classic line of monster-training adventures. Digimon has always felt a bit like Pokémon's darker and more dangerous cousin, but with Survive it's ditching both the cartoon style of the Digimon worlds and the sci-fi RPG action of the most recent Cyber Sleuth games. Instead, we've got something that's part adventure, part tactical RPG. Don't worry, though. Befriending and battling with magical creatures is still right at its core.

The game follows a group of teenagers lost on a school camping trip—and transported to a strange new world of monsters. There they partner up with friendly Digimon and try to work out what's happened to them. Can they survive in the Digimon world, and can they get back to the world they've lost?

QUICK TIPS:

BIG DECISIONS
■ The choices you make in the drama sections of the game change the story, and affect the battles you face and how your Digimon evolve.

LEARN YOUR DIGIMON
■ Your heroes will partner with different Digimon who have their own strengths and weaknesses. Play to each Digimon's strengths when they're in battle—and keep an eye on their health.

EVOLVE
■ Your Digimon can level up and evolve during combat, giving them new attacks and making them tougher. It will cost you energy, but you can refill your energy meter by beating other Digimon in battle.

DIGIMON: DANGER AND DRAMA

■ In Digimon Survive, you have to guide your heroes in battle and through the ongoing drama. They're ordinary kids trying to survive in a dangerous new world.

Minoru
Mysteriously disappeared, huh?
There's a lot of scary stories around here.

■ The drama sections split into two types. In the Free Action sections, you use the map to choose where to go and whom to talk to. By choosing an area and talking to your friends, you can find out more about them and what they need from you.

■ In the Search Action sections, you're thrown into a tricky or risky situation, and have to use your wits and Digimon friends to get through it. Can you survive the crisis? Get it wrong and the effects could be deadly!

FAST FACT:

Digimon Survive celebrates the 20th anniversary of the original TV show. Since then, we've had another six different Digimon series, though not all have been shown in the USA.

■ The Battle sections play out like a classic strategy RPG, where you take turns to move your Digimon and select their attacks. Position and movement are important. Don't let your Digimon get stranded or surrounded.

■ Each Digimon has its own powers with which it can attack enemy Digimon or heal Digimon on the home team. You can level up and evolve your Digimon in battle, so the more they fight, the stronger they'll become!

IT'S LIKE:
FIRE EMBLEM: THREE HOUSES
■ Your first thought might be Pokémon: Sword, but Digimon Survive's combat has more in common with Fire Emblem's tactical battles.

FIRE EMBLEM
THREE HOUSES

Temtem

TRY: TEMTEM
■ If you like exploring and battling with friendly monsters, Temtem is the massive multiplayer Poké-clone you've always dreamed of.

SUPER SMASH BROS.
ULTIMATE X
FIRE EMBLEM

It's an irresistible combination: Nintendo's mighty fighting game meets its unbeatable strategy RPG. Maybe that's why Super Smash Bros. Ultimate crammed six Fire Emblem heroes into its roster, then released a seventh—Byleth—as a DLC.

■ Previous Fire Emblem challengers have tended to be hard-hitting sword fighters. Chrom, from Fire Emblem: Awakening, is a classic example. He's a fast-moving warrior who rushes his enemies. His smashes pack a lot of power, and it's easy to build up massive-damage combos.

■ Byleth differs from most of the game's fighters. You can play the same character in either male or female versions, just like in Fire Emblem: Three Houses, and he or she can wield four different weapons, making Byleth a versatile fighter.

■ Marth and Lucina are very mobile, with speedy swordplay, and awesome dash and air moves. Watch your position, though. You've got to leave enough space for their Falchion blades to do maximum damage.

■ Byleth's big thing is range. She's not as fast as Chrom or as mobile as Marth, but she's got options that can help you smash your enemies from a distance. The Sword of the Creator works as a normal sword, but can also transform into a whip for longer range attacks, and for sweeping and juggling foes into the air.

■ The Aymr Axe has powerful downward swings, while the Areadbhar lance is perfect for keeping aggressive characters at a distance, though it's useless if they get in close. Luckily, you can quickly switch to another weapon by changing the direction of the stick when you tilt and attack.

■ Byleth also has the Failnaught Bow. You can charge up your arrows until you've got your opponent in your sights, then fire for extra damage.

FAST FACT:
Marth and Roy were so popular in 2001's Smash Bros. Melee that it persuaded Nintendo to release Fire Emblem games in the USA.

■ With Byleth comes the chance to battle on a stage based on the Garreg Mach monastery, along with alternative costumes based on the styles of the three house leaders—Dimitri, Edgelgard, and Claude. It's enough to turn any Smash fan into a full-on Fire Emblem fanatic!

DRAGON BALL Z: KAKAROT

FIGHT THROUGH THE WHOLE SAIYAN SAGA

28

32

Dragon Ball Z: Kakarot is huge! Where other games might have struggled to retell just one of the show's epic story arcs, Kakarot squeezes the whole Saiyan, Frieza, Cell, and Buu story lines into a single awesome action RPG. You play as Goku on his mission to rescue Gohan from his evil space uncle, and as Piccolo watching over Gohan as he trains. You can then play as Goku, Gohan, Piccolo, and Vegeta as they battle the Emperor Frieza. And that's just in the first two acts!

There's more to Kakarot than fighting, though. Between the massive set-piece battles, you've got time to wander around the game's different regions, collecting Z-Orbs, hunting and fishing, running small side missions, and grabbing ingredients to cook. There's even space for a driving lesson. No other Dragon Ball game has taken you this deep into the Dragon Ball universe, or given you so much time with its stars.

QUICK TIPS:

DON'T RUSH INTO BATTLE
■ Don't jump straight to the next big battle. Exploring and completing side-missions is fun, and you can level up your heroes and attacks. You'll need all the strength you can get for later dust ups.

TAKE TIME TO HEAL UP
■ Use the campfires to rest and eat between battles and regain your health. You can also carry items like Healade and Vitadrink to regain health during fights.

COLLECT Z-ORBS
■ Flying around and collecting Z-Orbs is no waste of time. You can spend them to develop and enhance more powerful super attacks.

Gohan

My name's Gohan.

EXPLORE THE WORLD OF DRAGON BALL Z

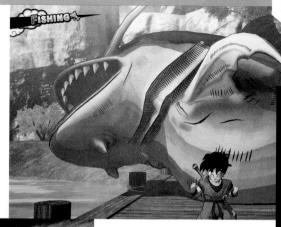

FISHING

COMPLETE THE SUB STORIES

■ Each area is packed with characters who'll have short "sub story" missions to complete. Polish these off between the big battles to get XP and upgrade your heroes.

FISH FOR YOUR SUPPER

■ Goku and Gohan can catch fish to make delicious, power-boosting meals. Just get that Saiyan tail in the water and wiggle it.

GO DRIVING

■ Sure, your heroes can fly around the world at supersonic speeds, but why not take it easy and go for a drive? You can even take part in races, but you'll need to pass your driving test first!

TRAIN TO WIN!

■ Later on, you'll unlock the training room, where you can unlock the hidden Mastery skill tree. This contains skills that can radically boost your attacks and help you take on two foes at a time.

GRAB A BITE

■ Hunt, fish, and search for ingredients, then find yourself a cook. Different meals will heal you and boost your abilities, so you're ready for your next fight.

COLLECT SOUL EMBLEMS

■ Make new friends and you'll get Soul Emblems, which you can pin to your Community Boards. Adding different Emblems to different Boards can make it easier to get great food, fight, or level up.

FAST FACT:

It would take you over seven days of continuous watching to get through the original Dragon Ball Z anime series. Completing Dragon Ball Z: Kakarot will take you at least 40 hours, and up to 100 if you try to do everything.

IT'S LIKE: DRAGON BALL XENOVERSE 2

■ Dragon Ball Z: Kakarot is much more of a story-driven RPG, but its exploration and combat come straight from the earlier Xenoverse games. Xenoverse 2 is still fantastic.

TRY: NARUTO SHIPPUDEN: ULTIMATE NINJA STORM 4

■ Looking for another video game take on a classic anime series? Ultimate Ninja Storm 4 covers the whole Naruto Shippuden story line in fist-smacking, fireball-flinging style.

DRAGON BALL Z: KAKAROT

SURVIVE THE SAIYAN SMACKDOWN!

Dragon Ball Z: Kakarot throws everything at its battles, making them the biggest, most spectacular bouts you've ever seen in a Dragon Ball game. With mid-air fights, huge Ki bursts and screen-filling energy beams, this isn't your average fighting game. If you want to win through to the next chapter of the story, you need to master all the different aspects of the combat—and that's Saiyan a lot!

FAST FACT:
Akira Toriyama, the artist behind Dragon Ball Z, is also famous for his character design on the Dragon Quest and Chrono Trigger games.

■ You stay locked on to your enemy, and hitting the Fight button repeatedly will have you charging into battle and stringing hits into a brutal combo. Finish off with a special move or super attack to bring down their health bar.

■ Hold the Block button to take the sting out of incoming attacks, or dodge fireballs and blasts if you can. One sneaky trick is to block when the enemy gets close, then blast them with a Ki Blast. It will send them flying. Just watch out or they might do the same to you!

Lvl 6 Raditz
7349
STUN

x5

COMBO
13

Lvl 2

Lvl 3 Goku
6066
101

■ In some battles, you can bring a friend! Press the Support button to call them in for a special combo move. You need help to bring these Saiyan bruisers to their knees.

■ Keep a very close eye on your health and Ki bars. If you're on the red bar and it's falling, you need to think about healing fast. You can recharge your Ki by holding down the Ki button—but not when you're being attacked.

■ All your heroes will also have super attacks, which you can get to by holding the L1 button or left bumper. Use them when your enemy is still or moving toward you to whack them for maximum damage.

114

Piccolo

Special Beam Cannon!

COMBO
5

Lvl 7 Piccolo

VALORANT

THE TEAM BEHIND LEAGUE OF LEGENDS HAS OVERWATCH IN ITS SIGHTS

Riot Games knows what it's doing with Multiplayer Online Battle Arena games. After all, it's the studio behind League of Legends. But does it have what it takes to take on Counter-Strike and Overwatch with a new competitive shooter? Play Valorant and you might be surprised to find the answer. Yes, it does!

This is a shooter with serious appeal for eSports fans, doing everything it can to push pure shooting skills and strategy over cheap, sneaky tricks. It's as fast-paced and exciting as the old-school shooters like Call of Duty or Counter-Strike. Yet, it also packs in the heroes and unique abilities of a game like Overwatch, as players join a group of agents working to arm or defuse bombs. Each agent has his or her own amazing gadgets or powers, designed to confuse, surprise, or hide from the other team, giving your guys the chance to grab a tactical advantage.

QUICK TIPS:

AWESOME AGENTS
■ Try all the different agents and work out which one fits your play style. Each one has two unique gadgets or abilities, allowing you to play different offensive, defensive, or support roles.

GO IN GUNS BLAZING
■ Your abilities are important, but they're no substitute for fast reflexes and a great aim. Even though this is a hero shooter, you'll get most of your eliminations with a gun.

UPGRADE YOUR WEAPONS
■ Make sure you use the opportunity to buy new weapons at the start of every round. Keep upgrading to bigger, better guns to stay ahead of the enemy.

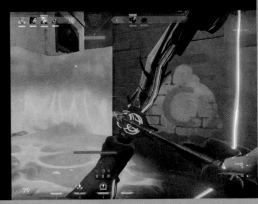

PROVE YOUR VALOR

THE BASICS
■ Valorant is a tactical shooter played by two teams of five players. Whichever team wins the most of 25 rounds comes out with the win.

ATTACK AND DEFENCE
■ One team is attacking, trying to plant an explosive device called the Spike. They have to plant the Spike in one of three set positions, then protect it until it explodes. The other team has to stop them or defuse the Spike before it blows!

FIGHT TO SURVIVE
■ There's no respawning in Valorant. If you're killed, you have to wait until the next round before you can join in again. If you want new guns, you have to purchase them at the start of every round with the credits you've earned so far.

AGENT ABILITIES
■ All the agents have their own powers. For instance, Phoenix can throw fireballs and blinding flares or create a flame wall that blocks enemy vision. Jett can create a fog or dash upward or forward at high speeds. Other agents specialize in poisonous gadgets, traps, or drones.

TRACK THEM DOWN
■ Many agent abilities are designed for scouting, targeting, and recon, enabling you to find enemy agents behind walls or inside buildings, or target an agent even when they're hidden by a cloud of fog.

FAST FACT:
Riot has one of the world's biggest games in League of Legends, with over 80 million active players and up to 8 million playing at any time!

IT'S LIKE: OVERWATCH
■ Valorant has a lot in common with Overwatch, but it's less about the hero powers and more about the gunplay.

TRY: SHADOWGUN WAR GAMES
■ Looking for a mobile hero shooter? Give Shadowgun War Games a spin. It's a bit of an Overwatch clone, but the best you'll get on your tablet or smartphone.

NO CONSOLE?
NO PROBLEM!

You don't need a games machine to play the biggest games

■ If you've wanted to game, you've always needed great hardware, which meant spending big bucks on a console or an expensive, powerful PC. What's more, to play the best games, you've always needed a specific console. Want to play Halo, Forza, and Sea of Thieves? You're going to need an Xbox One. Meanwhile, Marvel's Spider-Man, Horizon: Zero Dawn, and Final Fantasy VII Remake are off the menu if you don't have a PS4.

■ Now this is changing, and it's all because of the Internet tech and online services that make up what we call "the cloud." With the new breed of "cloud gaming services," you don't need a console or a hugely expensive PC. You just need a cheap laptop or Chromebook with a browser, or even a tablet, smartphone, or video streaming device. As long as you've got a controller and a speedy Internet connection, you've got games.

Project xCloud
[P R E V I E W]
Play 50+ Xbox games on your mobile phone or tablet

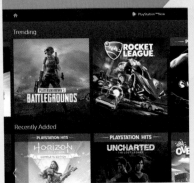

HOW DOES CLOUD GAMING WORK?

■ With a normal console or gaming PC, the console takes code from the game software and turns it into the amazing 3D graphics you see on your TV. Other code controls how the game world behaves, or what the other characters in the game are doing, and how they will react to the player.

■ Meanwhile, the console is bringing in information from your controller to work out things like where you're moving, what you're aiming at, or how far you're going to jump. The console might also be taking the same information from other players you're playing over the Internet, so that you can all play together at the same time.

■ With cloud gaming, all this work is being done by a computer, miles away and connected to the Internet. It takes in what you're doing with your controller, so that it understands where you're going and what you're trying to do, and it sends back a stream of sound and video that plays in your browser or on your TV. This happens so quickly and so smoothly that it feels like you're playing your game on a console in the same room.

WHAT'S GOOD ABOUT CLOUD GAMING?

YOU DON'T NEED A CONSOLE

■ You don't have to spend $400 to $500 on a new console every few years. Instead, you (or your parents) pay $10 or so a month for a subscription. This might include a library of games you can play. You might even find that, while you pay for the games, the service itself is free!

SHORTER LOADING TIMES

■ With some cloud gaming services, you don't have to wait while the game loads onto a console—you connect to a computer that's already set up to run it. All it needs to do is load your saved game, and you're up and playing in minutes.

NO DISCS, DOWNLOADS, OR UPDATES

■ You don't need to get a disc or download the game, and you don't need to wait two hours for the latest update to download and install.

PLAY WHERE YOU LIKE

■ With cloud gaming, you're no longer stuck playing on your console in the living room. Going away for the weekend? You can play the same game on your smartphone and carry on exactly where you left off.

WHAT'S NOT SO GOOD?

YOU NEED A GOOD INTERNET CONNECTION

■ Cloud gaming works on most Internet connections, but if yours is slow or goes in and out, games might not be playable. The graphics could go horrible and blocky.

GRAPHICS QUALITY

■ If you're used to playing games on an Xbox One, PS4, or Switch, then games running on a cloud service won't look much different. If you've got a 4K TV and an Xbox One, PS4 Pro, or PC, then the games might not look as good.

HUNGRY FOR DATA

■ Cloud gaming services use a lot of data, and if you don't have an "unlimited" Internet connection, you could end up using your family's monthly data plan over a weekend. Will they be happy about that? Probably not.

CONTENDER ONE:
GOOGLE STADIA

■ Stadia comes from the same people who brought you the Google search engine, Chromebooks, Android, and a whole lot more. It runs on computers that are—in theory—even more powerful than the Xbox One X, so games can look amazing on a 4K TV set, as long as your Internet connection is really fast.

■ Stadia actually gives you two options. If you pay $10 a month for the Stadia Pro service, you can play games in 4K, and you get at least one free game to play every month that you're subscribed. You have to pay for other games, and they cost you roughly what you'd pay for the same game on Xbox One or PS4.

■ However, there's also a free Stadia Base service, where you can play only at a lower full HD resolution and you don't get the free games. This doesn't sound great, but you can still buy games and play them without spending on a new console. That doesn't sound like a bad deal to us.

WHAT DO YOU NEED?

■ Google makes its own Stadia controller and you can use a Google Chromecast Ultra streamer to play games through your TV. However, you can use other controllers—including Xbox One and PS4 controllers— and play through a browser on a standard laptop. You can also play Stadia on some Android tablets and smartphones, including Google's own Pixel phones.

WHAT CAN YOU PLAY?

■ Stadia's library of games is growing, and you can already play games like Destiny 2, Final Fantasy XV, Dragon Ball Xenoverse 2, Marvel's Avengers, Gods & Monsters, and NBA 2K20. You won't find the full range of games you'll find on consoles, though.

WHAT'S IT LIKE?

■ Stadia works amazingly well on the right connection, and you can connect up for a quick game of Destiny 2 within a minute. However, you need a fast Internet connection to get the best 4K graphics. Stadia's library also needs more games, and it's disappointing when they cost more on Stadia than they do on the Xbox One or PS4.

CONTENDER TWO:
MICROSOFT XCLOUD

■ Microsoft xCloud is part of Microsoft's Xbox gaming system, and it's designed to stream Xbox games to smartphones, tablets, and low-power laptops over Wi-Fi or a mobile Internet connection. The games run on computers that are basically a bunch of modified Xbox One S consoles working together.

■ As a result, xCloud games don't run at the same resolutions and graphics settings as they might on the Xbox One S or Xbox One X consoles, but they still run in high definition and look incredible on your smartphone.

■ This cloud gaming service works hand in hand with Microsoft's Xbox Games Pass, where you pay a monthly subscription to play a library of games, including big Microsoft favorites like Forza Horizon 4 and Halo 5: Guardians. In the future, you might also be able to play other Xbox games you own, even when you're nowhere near your console!

WHAT DO YOU NEED?

■ Just a smartphone, tablet, or computer that can run the xCloud app and an Xbox One controller. The app works on a range of Android smartphones and Windows 10 computers, with more to come.

WHAT CAN YOU PLAY?

■ A good selection of Microsoft exclusives and Xbox Games Pass favorites, so the Halo and Forza games, the two Ori titles, Sea of Thieves, ReCore, and Killer Instinct are all there for you to enjoy. Lots of other companies have also jumped onboard, so you can play WWE 2K20, Overcooked, Yoku's Island Express, and F1 2019 as well. We'd expect all Xbox Games Pass games to be available eventually.

WHAT'S IT LIKE?

■ You don't get the full 4K graphics of Xbox One X or Stadia, and you might find a tiny bit of lag: a split-second delay between you pressing a button on your controller and the action happening. This varies from game to game. Overall, though, you can play Halo 5, Sea of Thieves, or Ori on your smartphone, and it looks and feels great. Love Xbox? You'll love this—and it opens up Xbox games to a whole new audience!

CONTENDER THREE:
PLAYSTATION NOW

■ PlayStation Now was one of the first cloud gaming services to launch, where it started off streaming PS2 and PS3 games. In the last few years, it's taken on PS4 games as well, including some of Sony's biggest hits. It's not as flexible as Stadia or xCloud, though, as it only runs on PS4 consoles and Windows PCs.

■ On PS4, you can choose to download the games instead of streaming them, while on PC it's streaming only. There's also no way right now to run PlayStation Now on a phone or tablet. The biggest plus is that, as with the Xbox Games Pass, you can stream or download any game in the library for free, making it a great way to try out games.

WHAT CAN YOU PLAY?

■ A strong selection of games from PS2, PS3, and PS4, including many Sony classics. There's not always so much for younger gamers, and Sony has a nasty habit of making its biggest and best PS4 games only available for a few months at a time—bad news if you come back later to finish it off and find it gone. Still, with games as good as Rocket League, Overcooked, Steep, LittleBigPlanet 3, and a whole bunch of Sonic and Star Wars games, it's hard to complain.

WHAT'S IT LIKE?

■ Streaming works well on PlayStation Now, though it struggles more with slow connections than xCloud or Stadia. Sony's games library could do with an update, though, and it's going to be interesting to see how things evolve with PlayStation 5.

WHAT DO YOU NEED?

■ A PS4, PS4 Pro, or Windows 10 PC and a Dual Shock 4 controller. If you have a PS Plus subscription, you can transfer your saved games from your PS4 to PlayStation Now using the cloud. That's great when you want to carry on where you left off.

PlayStation™ Now

LittleBigPlanet™ 3
PS4 ★★★★☆ (23505)

PLAYSTATION HITS

Join Sackboy® and his amazing team of new friends on a wild adventure across a mysterious, unexplored world packed with endless surprises.

Start

Your List

Sony Interactive Entertainment Europe

Enter   Cancel   Health & Terms

CLOUD GAMING: THE FUTURE

■ Some people in the games business think that cloud gaming is the future. We'll no longer have to buy consoles or gaming PCs to play the latest hits, but just fire up a browser on any device and connect straight to the game or to a Netflix-style service. When you play a game like Destiny 2 on Stadia or connect to PlayStation Now, this doesn't sound unrealistic. Still, not everyone sees things the same way.

■ For example, Phil Spencer, the head of Xbox, has said that while cloud gaming will be part of the future, it's not going to replace consoles any time soon. This is why Microsoft is still focusing on big, powerful consoles like the Xbox Series X for gaming when you're at home on your TV, but hoping you'll use xCloud to take the games with you when you leave the living room.

SECOND OPINION

Rob Leane is the Editor-in-Chief of StealthOptional.com, a tech and gaming website

■ Streaming from the cloud is one of the most exciting new things in gaming. You don't need a console or a powerful computer to play big games. If a game that you want to try out can be streamed—and your internet connection is up to the job—give game streaming a try and feel just how futuristic it is! When I was reviewing Google Stadia, I couldn't believe that my old laptop could play such massive games—it feels like high-tech magic! And if it means people who can't afford to buy snazzy consoles can join in with the joy of gaming, what's not to love?

MADDEN NFL

THIS ONE'S FOR THE SUPERSTAR PLAYERS

Every year there's a new Madden, and every year EA Sports has to deliver an exciting, new feature to make this year's version better or more realistic than the last. With Madden 20, it came up with a winner: superstar players and their unique X-Factor abilities.

These transform games by turning each quarter into a thriller. Can your superstar players hit the objectives they need to unlock their X-Factor? An X-Factor can mean the difference between a play that goes absolutely nowhere and one that makes it to the end zone. An X-Factor could mean winning a crucial catch or stopping a powerhouse offensive play in its tracks.

Throw in more realistic movement, passing, and tackles, and you have a game that's only getting more exciting—and can make you feel like a superstar player yourself!

QUICK TIPS:

SWITCH TACTICS

■ Some of the old Madden tactics aren't as effective as they used to be. You need to get the ball moving faster or you'll get sacked in many plays, and you can't rely on your linebackers to get you out of trouble.

TRAIN UP

■ Recent changes, like Run Pass Option plays, take some getting used to. Use the Skills Trainer in the Exhibition menu, and try running through the new playbooks.

MASTER THE MISSIONS

■ Madden Ultimate Team mode can be hard to get into, but taking on the Missions will give you a guided way in and introduce all the basics. It's the best way to get to grips with the game.

THIS IS FOOTBALL!

WIN THE ONE-ON-ONES
■ What good is a throw if you can't win the ball? The Buccaneers' Mike Evans Double Me X-Factor uses his size and superhuman tracking to increase his success rate on aggressive catches.

THROW LONGER
■ X-Factor moves can make or break a game. The Chiefs' Patrick Mahomes Bazooka X-Factor gives him a huge maximum throwing distance that can force the ball through the toughest defense.

KICKS AND CONVERSIONS
■ Madden has gotten smarter about how it handles kicks and conversions. As you get closer to the goalposts, you can focus less on power and more on accuracy.

FAST FACT:
The Madden NFL series is one of the biggest in gaming history, with well over 130 million copies sold. For the last 20 years, it's been the bestselling game in the month of its release!

RUNS AND PASSES
■ The way Madden handles running plays and passes has also loosened up, giving you more space for strong plays to break through the defensive lines.

YOU'VE GOT OPTIONS
■ This goes double when it comes to Run Pass Option plays. Giving quarterbacks the option to hand the ball off or throw a quick pass—or even make the run themselves—makes things really tough for the defense.

IT'S LIKE: MADDEN NFL 19
■ Since 2K Games dropped the NFL 2K series, Madden NFL has become the only football game in town. NFL 19 plays a solid game of football, but the newer games are so much better!

TRY: MLB THE SHOW 20
■ Would you rather play baseball? PS4 exclusive MLB The Show is the way to go, playing a brilliant, lifelike game of baseball that looks and feels like the real thing.

Images captured from PS4 Pro System

FIFA

FIFA'S TAKING SOCCER TO THE STREETS

Despite tough competition from Konami's Pro Evolution Soccer, FIFA is still the biggest and best soccer game around. It has all the modes and all the teams, and it plays an incredibly realistic version of the beautiful game. But that doesn't mean it can't use a shake-up. Enter the new Volta mode, taking a faster, less rules-heavy game of soccer out of the stadium and onto the streets.

Beyond Volta, FIFA has everything a soccer fan could wish for, including an in-depth career mode, some of the world's biggest tournaments, and the legendary FIFA Ultimate Team mode. Whether you want to take on your friends online or build a dream team of the world's finest players, FIFA has you covered. Best of all, there's a real sense of pace to the latest version, and with enhancements to the defensive game and shooting, it's playing better than it ever has before.

QUICK TIPS:

TIMING IS EVERYTHING
■ Timed finishing is crucial to scoring goals. Tap the shoot button quickly after you've taken the shot and it's more likely to reach the net, but tap it too early or too late and you could make it worse.

JOCKEY FOR THE BALL
■ Instead of trying to pull off unlikely tackles, try using the jockey controls (L2 and R2) to block shots and intercept passes.

DRILLS FOR SKILLS
■ Head to Skill Games on the main menu to get some practice with the new game mechanics and controls. It's the best way to master FIFA and play like a star.

VIVA VOLTA!

TELL YOUR STORY
■ Volta has its own story mode, where you create your own player and join an up-and-coming team as they fight to make it onto the global street soccer stage.

MIXING IT UP
■ Volta teams mix male and female players, and they'll use a huge range of different skills. Don't worry if you're not an expert—hold down both triggers and your player will use smart autoskills.

STREET SOCCER
■ Volta is all about taking FIFA away from the big clubs and superstar players, and bringing it down to street level, for an even faster, more dynamic game.

DIFFERENT STYLES
■ Matches play out in different pitch areas on different surfaces, which makes the action even more intense. You'll also play with different team sizes. Some don't have anyone in goal!

SMALLER TARGETS
■ Smaller pitches mean smaller goals, which means you have to be a whole lot more accurate with your shooting. Still, some matches do without the boundaries, so you can't kick the ball off the field!

FAST FACT:
Volta means to return in Portuguese, which makes sense as it's a return to the back-to-basics street-style soccer of the FIFA Street games, which last appeared in 2012.

TRY: ROCKET LEAGUE
■ Think soccer would be more exciting if played by rocket-powered cars? You're in luck! Play it and you'll soon find out why Rocket League is a phenomenon.

IT'S LIKE: PES 2020
■ Konami's FIFA rival came out beautiful but broken, although fixes have made it a stronger game. FIFA is the soccer champ right now, but don't be surprised if PES makes a comeback.

NBA 2K

SWISH, ANOTHER ONE IN THE BASKET

QUICK TIPS:

STUDY THE GAME
■ Make the most of the 2KU tutorial mode. It will teach you all the basic skills and some advanced ones—and remind you of stuff you might have forgotten since last year's game.

CREATE SPACE
■ Defenders will close ranks and wall up on you if you just storm toward the basket. Use passing plays to create space for your best shooters to take their shot.

MARK THEM CLOSELY
■ While it's tempting to keep switching players while defending, try focusing on your current player and who they're marking. Watch their indicators and, when they move, try to block them.

L ike its 2K20 cover star, the Lakers' Anthony Davis, 2K's basketball series seems unstoppable. In fact, for the last few years, it's wiped out all competition! That comes down to a core court game that's fast, fluid, and furiously addictive, and the authenticity that rolls into every area of the game, from the presentation to the different career modes.

The latest versions have taken this further than ever before, so that on top of the MyLeague, MyTeam, and MyCareer modes, we now get the WNBA with all 12 teams plus stars like Candace Parker and Elena Delle Donne represented. And while it's been tough, the on-court action has improved as well, so that players dribble with their own unique style and no longer seem to be skating around. Can the best basketball game get better? You'd better believe it can!

THE BEST GETS BETTER

ON THE COURT

■ NBA 2K has fixed player movement on the court and changed how dribbling is animated, to make it look incredibly convincing. Off-ball moves also return— and they're smarter than ever!

BECOME AN NBA LEGEND

■ The MyCareer mode is back with an epic storyline featuring stars Idris Elba and Rosario Dawson. You can create and follow your rookie player as they try to make it big in the NBA.

PLAY WNBA

■ The 12 teams of the WNBA are included, giving you a slightly different style of basketball. Playing this single-season mode is a great way to get your head around the changes in NBA 2K.

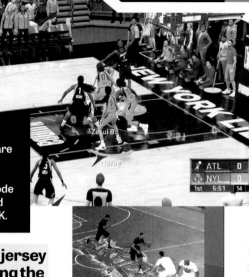

FAST FACT:

Wondering why Anthony Davis wears an unmarked jersey on the 2K20 cover? It was shot in-between him leaving the New Orleans Pelicans and moving to LA to join the Lakers.

SET YOUR POTENTIAL

PLAY TO YOUR STRENGTHS

■ The player creation and customization options are unbelievable. Tweak your player to make them the ultimate shooter or playmaker, then earn the badges that will boost their skills through the roof.

HIT THE BLACKTOP

■ The BlackTop mode gives you a more casual, street style of play featuring one-man to five-man teams. It's perfect for trying out new skills with your pick of the NBA's top players.

IT'S LIKE: NBA LIVE 19

■ EA Sports' last attempt at an NBA Live comeback was easier to get into than the recent NBA2K games, but even a focus on street basketball couldn't knock 2K's game off the throne.

TRY: NHL 20

■ Looking for another fast-paced sports sim with all-action gameplay and amazing graphics? NHL 20 is the best hockey game in years.

PLAYST

Fifteen all-time PlayStation greats you can still play today

PLAY IT:
Everybody's Golf is the latest PS4 version, but you can play World Invitational on PSNow

PLAY IT:
Try the superb PS4 remake or A Crack in Time and Quest for Booty on PSNow

2002
RATCHET & CLANK

■ PlayStation has had its share of platform game mascots, but we reckon Ratchet & Clank come number one. You've got to love the alien mechanic and his wisecracking robot pal, and the games have packed in some of the most ingenious contraptions and imaginative worlds across PS2, PS3, and PS4. There's lots of leaping, shooting, and puzzle-solving to be done, with weird and wonderful weapons and gadgets galore.

2011
HOT SHOTS GOLF: WORLD INVITATIONAL

■ You might think golf is as boring as sports come, but Hot Shots Golf says different. This series has always been bright, breezy, and fun to pick up and play, and World Invitational is its best-ever version. There's a great balance between the cartoon graphics of the early games and lifelike detail in the scenery. The courses hit just the right level of challenge, and the game still has a silly side, with power-ups to use and crazy costumes to unlock. Trust us, you'll love it!

PLAY IT:
Grab the PS4 remake from the PlayStation Store or take the trip on PSNow

2012

JOURNEY

■ There were great indie games before Journey, but this game took it to a whole new level. It was arty, clever, and packed with smart ideas, but it also looked and felt like an epic, despite a short three-to-four hour running time. Your childlike hero explores magnificent ruins that come alive when activated, then faces scary monsters and impossible climbs. The visuals and the music create something really special, with a unique, silent approach to online co-op play.

CLASSICS

PLAY IT:
Leap into Ico's strange world in the HD remaster on PSNow

ICO

2001

■ When Ico arrived in 2001, nobody had seen anything like it. Sure, it was an action-adventure game where a boy explored a huge, haunted castle, but it had a style and a story that seemed to have come from another world. The game—with our young hero working to help a mysterious girl escape the castle, saving her from phantoms and dealing with obstacles—creates more tension, drama, and excitement than most games before or since.

MOTORSTORM: APOCALYPSE

2011

PLAY IT:
Get into the driver's seat on PSNow

2001 to 2008

■ You could describe MotorStorm as the defining racing series for the PS3, with its mud-churning, rough and tumble racing and awesome graphics. Each of the three games was great, but Apocalypse took the series to a whole new place. Not only are you racing thugs on cars, bikes, monster trucks, and ATVs, but you're speeding through a collapsing city in the middle of earthquakes and tornadoes. A white-knuckle roller coaster of an off-road racer.

BURNOUT

■ OK, we're going to cheat by going for a series rather than a single game, but only because just one game from this brilliant racing series is still available—and it's the PS3's Burnout Paradise. The original Burnout first amped the racing game with its killer combo of high speeds, traffic-dodging, and spectacular crashes, and by 2005's Burnout Revenge it was perfected. Burnout Paradise then went the extra mile by taking the action open world.

PLAY IT:
Drive angry in Burnout Paradise: Remastered from the PlayStation Store

LITTLEBIGPLANET

■ Media Molecule, the team behind Dreams, made their name with this adorable 2D platformer, where everything seems to be handcrafted from felt, tinfoil, and cardboard. Even its heroes, the lovable sackboy or sackgirl, look like they'd been stitched together from scraps. But the real joy of LittleBigPlanet is that you can take all these bits and make your own worlds, with your own heroes, villains, and adventures. Creative gaming at its best.

2008

PLAY IT:
You can't play the original on PS4, but LittleBigPlanet 3 is made of the exact same stuff

CRASH BANDICOOT

■ Naughty Dog built its reputation on this early PlayStation blockbuster, showing that it wasn't just Nintendo that could make a 3D platform game work. In fact, the first Crash Bandicoot mixed conventional 2D levels with crazy 3D chase sequences, but the speed of the action and the game's outrageous cartoon style made it an early must-have for the console. Two further platform games and a kart racer followed, and they're all worth playing.

PLAY IT:
Grab hold of the Crash Bandicoot N. Sane Trilogy remake from the PlayStation Store

CASTLEVANIA: SYMPHONY OF THE NIGHT

1997

PLAY IT:
Bite into the fang-tastic Castlevania: Requiem bundle on the PlayStation Store

■ Just when the biggest names in games were obsessed with making their blockbusters work in 3D, Konami decided to use the power of PlayStation to make one incredibly ambitious 2D game. Castlevania: Symphony of the Night is a vampire-hunting epic, set in a sprawling, shifting castle full of wonders. New powers unlock new areas and allow you to battle even more challenging monsters in a game that's still influencing modern hits like Dead Cells and Hollow Knight.

2001

JAK AND DAXTER: THE PRECURSOR LEGACY

■ Between Crash Bandicoot and Uncharted, Naughty Dog created a brilliant series of PS2 platformers that owed as much to The Legend of Zelda as they did Mario. In the first, Jak, a sci-fi elf, and his buddy, Daxter, a long-eared, weasel-like critter, explore the game's lush open world in search of mysterious, ancient technology. There's plenty of platforming, fighting, and even racing to be done. While the rest of the trilogy takes a different turn, the quality never takes a dive.

PLAY IT:
Track down all the Jak and Daxter games, remastered, on the PlayStation Store

WIPEOUT

1995

■ Tekken and Crash Bandicoot were something else, but nothing defined PlayStation more than Wipeout. A stupidly fast, incredibly intense sci-fi racing game, it featured stomach-churning roller coaster tracks and a soundtrack crammed with the coolest electronic dance music of the time. This made Wipeout irresistible to everyone from 10 to 30, even though the difficulty level was as fierce as they come. The series has reappeared on every PlayStation since.

PLAY IT:
Wipeout Omega Collection is a Wipeout greatest hits. Grab it from the PlayStation Store

OKAMI

2006

■ Launching just as the PS3 was released, Okami proved the PS2 still had some gas in the tank. It's a stunning Japanese adventure, where the ink-and-paper graphics aren't just for show—you fight the game's monsters with swiping brushstrokes across the screen, while you know areas of the world are cured of demonic infection when they blossom into color. With its mystic mutt hero, oddball characters, and magical landscapes, this is the best Zelda that Nintendo never made.

PLAY IT:
The magnificent HD remaster can be found on the PlayStation Store

FINAL FANTASY XII

2006

■ We could half-fill this list with Final Fantasy games. How about the groundbreaking Final Fantasy VII, or the underappreciated Final Fantasy IX? The PS2 era brought us Final Fantasy X and X-2, with their dazzling sci-fi sagas, and even Final Fantasy VIII and XIII have their fans. You owe it to yourself to play this year's Final Fantasy VII Remake, but for us the high point of the series has to be Final Fantasy XII. Released at the end of the PS2 era, it's a huge RPG set in an exotic fantasy world, with lovable heroes, evil villains, and a brilliant battle system that makes it easy to manage your squad of sorcerers and fighters. It's a high point in a series full of classics, and if you haven't played it, you should.

PLAY IT:
Find the Final Fantasy XII The Zodiac Age remaster on the PlayStation Store

TEKKEN

1995

■ Tekken was a crucial game for the original PlayStation console, showcasing its awesome graphics power at a time when fighting games were absolutely massive. It also helped define the 3D fighting game, taking what Sega had done with Virtua Fighter, but adding crazy storylines, fantasy characters, and brutal special moves. Its dark and edgy style helped bring console gaming to a different audience, and the series is still going strong today.

PLAY IT:
You can't play the classic Tekkens on PS4, but Tekken Tag Tournament 2 is on PSNow

SHADOW OF THE COLOSSUS

2005

■ Team Ico followed up Ico with a game even more strange and beautiful. A young man on horseback enters an abandoned land filled with strange ruins, carrying the lifeless body of a young girl. To bring her back to life, he must find, climb, and kill 16 massive creatures—the colossi. The world, its landscapes, and its creatures, including the colossi, are works of art, and if each frame looks like a painting, each colossal battle is a stomach-churning thrill ride.

PLAY IT:
Slay the giants on PSNow or play the superb PS4 remaster

SNOWRUNNER

Big trucks, off-road action, hair-raising slopes, water, mud, and ice: all the ingredients for some tough trucking drama, as you drive vital supplies cross-country to the people who need them most. SnowRunner is the sequel to the cult classic Spintires: MudRunner, which gave us a driving game that wasn't about winning races, but about pulling heavy loads across impossible terrain with your ever-growing fleet of vehicles.

SnowRunner doubles down on the same ideas, but spreads them out across massive maps based in Michigan, Russia, and Alaska. On top of chewing up the mud and scrambling along rocky roads, you'll now be pushing through thick snow and skidding on the ice. Switch to low gear, work the gas pedal, and hope you get some traction. In the nearest gaming gets to *Ice Road Truckers*, you face some tricky roads ahead.

QUICK TIPS:

USE THE WINCH

■ Are you stuck in thick snow or mud with your tires spinning? Try using a winch if you have one or bring another truck with one equipped. Just attach it to something solid and pull your truck free.

PICK THE RIGHT VEHICLE

■ If you can't move for the mud or you're struggling in the snow, you're probably not in the right vehicle or packing the right equipment. Switch trucks if you can or come back later with another vehicle.

STICK TO DAYTIME DRIVING

■ Driving at night gets really difficult, especially if you have to head off-road. Use the option to speed up time and wait for daylight before you head out on a tricky mission.

TRACTION HEROES

COLLECT YOUR CARGO

■ Most of the missions involve picking up materials from one place and driving them to another. You can pack your cargo automatically or winch it onto your truck yourself.

REACH YOUR DESTINATION

■ Once you're loaded up, the challenge is to get the cargo to the destination in one piece. Work out your route and use your trucking skills to get past any obstacles in your way.

BUILD YOUR FLEET

■ SnowRunner has over 40 vehicles to unlock, giving you the trucks you need to get through some of the world's harshest wilderness, including raging rivers, rocky slopes, and frozen lakes.

FAST FACT:

SnowRunner's largest maps are four times the size of MudRunner's biggest areas, and it has over 40 vehicles to unlock

DRIVE TO SURVIVE

■ You've got to master your truck driving skills and use your head to meet each challenge. How can you use your gears, off-road equipment, winch, and momentum to tackle roads that would destroy a normal vehicle?

IT'S LIKE: OVERPASS

■ Overpass is another off-road challenge game that's come out in the wake of Spintires: MudRunner. Just watch out for its fiendish difficulty level.

TRY: DIRT 4

■ Would you rather drive off-road at terrifying speeds? You can't do much better than Codemaster's DiRT series, with DiRT 4 one of the easiest rally racers to get into.

ROBLOX: OWN THE OBBY

It's hard to resist a good Roblox Obstacle Course, or Obby, but not everyone finds them easy. Do you struggle with the jumps or the disappearing platforms? Are exploding mines and killer obstacles causing you to fail? Don't panic! We can help with a few handy hints.

Here, we're using The Really Easy Obby! by GFink, but the same tricks will work on many other Obbies.

INVISIBLE PLATFORMS

■ Platforms and stairs that turn invisible can be tricky, but you can get through if you don't rush. Move when the blocks are visible, then pause as soon as they turn transparent. Wait until they become visible, then move again. With practice, you'll get better at judging how far you can move, but until that happens, take it slow!

MOVING PLATFORMS

■ This section is all about timing. The platform keeps moving, and you have to dodge left and right to avoid the red pillars, then jump over the hurdles on the floor. Using Shift-Lock can help you dodge smoothly left and right, but make sure you jump at the right points.

KILLER MINES

■ Dodging mines and other floor-based traps is a challenge, but you can do it if you watch for the areas where you have more space to move and take it slow! In this stage, using Shift-Lock and moving sideways can also help, as you're thinner moving sideways than walking forward or backward.

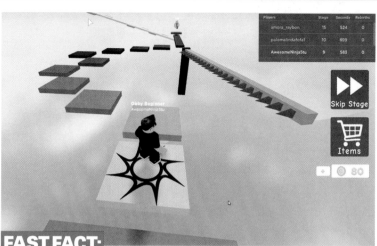

ROTATING DEATHTRAPS

■ You definitely don't want to get whacked by that rotating, spikey bar. Instead, wait until it moves past you and—without any pause or hesitation—hop around from platform to platform behind it. This is where you need tight mouse or right-stick skills to keep moving the view behind you as you jump.

FAST FACT:

There are more than 100 million Roblox players—or Robloxians—around the world, and more than two million of them have created a Roblox game.

SPEED TRIALS

■ In this section, the platforms disappear as you run across them—and you haven't got much time before you're falling to your doom! Move fast and look for shortcuts. You don't have to get right to the end of the blue platform before jumping onto the round, green platform.

SHIFT-LOCK

■ There are times in any Obby where you need precise movement, or a sideways step or jump to avoid an obstacle. Here, Shift-Lock is your new best friend. Head to the Settings tab on the menu to activate it. Now, tapping the Shift key or the up or down button on your D-Pad will lock your view in place, and you'll move sideways left or right just by pressing the left/right buttons, or A and D if you use a keyboard. Trust us, using Shift-Lock will make your Obby life easier.

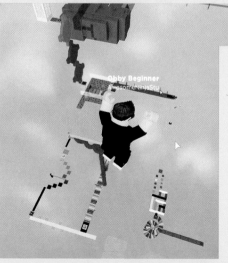

SPRING PADS

■ Here, each platform you land on propels you high into the air, and it's easy to miss the next platform and take a fatal fall. The trick is to bounce once on each platform without touching the movement keys or the left stick, and use the mouse or right stick to point yourself toward the next one. Bounce again, and you can press forward to land exactly where you need to.

BALANCE THE BIKE

■ Learn how to balance the bike, and how to lean back when you're jumping and forward when you land. Go too far or blow your timing, and you'll end up in a tumble, but it's the only way to win!

REWIND YOUR MISTAKES

■ The rewind button is your new best friend, especially when you're getting used to the game. Hit R1 or the right bumper to rewind back to a point before you failed the jump or skidded off the track.

GET A FAST START

■ For a quicker start, lean forward, hold the clutch button, squeeze the throttle, then release the clutch as the gate goes down. Hitting the first corner early gives you a big advantage.

MONSTER ENERGY SUPERCROSS

THE OFFICIAL VIDEOGAME 3

ALL THE THRILLS AND SPILLS OF AMERICA'S CRAZIEST MOTORSPORT

Forget that mouthful of a title. You're going to need all your energy and more to tame these two-wheeled beasts. This is the sport where 22 riders race one another on dirt courses crammed with bumps and jumps, and it's only skill between you and the next bone-breaking bailout. This is a tough game, but you will get better, and once you master its tricks of speed and balance, it's one satisfying mud-slinging racer.

Monster Energy Supercross the third has all the tracks and riders of the last Supercross season across three classes, covering the 250cc East and West divisions and the high-powered bikes of the 450SX. You can play through the 2019 championship or start your own career in Supercross, and for the first time race as either a male or female rider. Perhaps the most useful new addition is the all-new, bigger compound. Here, you can speed around pulling wheelies to your heart's content while you master the handling. That won't happen overnight!

BECOME A SUPERCROSS SUPERSTAR

MOTORBIKE MAYHEM
■ Be patient. This is one of the world's most manic motorsports, and even just making it around the track can be a challenge. With 22 other riders speeding and jumping around you, it's even tougher.

HIT THE COMPOUND
■ Rather than try to learn while you race, hit the compound and get a feel for the bikes and basic techniques. Learn how to balance, accelerate, brake, and corner.

TOUGH CONDITIONS
■ This third game in the series gives you a much better sense of how the tires are gripping in the dirt, but this also takes some getting used to, especially when rain turns all that dirt track to mud.

THREE CLASSES
■ Just when you've finally gotten used to the 250cc bikes of the first two classes, you'll move on to the 450SX class. Here, the bikes are more powerful, the turns will feel tighter, and you might have a hard time staying on!

MAKE TRACKS
■ Want a change? Why not build your own courses? The game features a built-in editor, where you can sculpt your own tracks full of jumps, bumps, and fiendish turns.

FAST FACT:
The new compound is based on the real-life Supercross Test Area in California, where the biggest racing teams put their bikes and riders through their paces.

IT'S LIKE: MXGP 2019
■ The Monster Energy Supercross series comes from the same developer as the official game of European motorcross. MXGP has more outdoor tracks, giving you a chance to get outside the stadiums and race.

TRY: WRECKFEST
■ If you'd rather play a less serious racer, take Wreckfest out for a spin. It's all about crazy off-road racing and demolition derbies in rusty, patched-up cars.

NEED FOR SPEED HEAT

IF YOU CAN'T TAKE THE HEAT, STAY OFF THE STREET

Palm City after dark is something else. By day, Need for Speed Heat's take on Miami hosts a street racing festival, where you can earn "bank" competing in legal races on special courses cleared of cars. By night, you take to the streets, building up your "rep" by racing against the city's crews in illegal sprint and circuit races. Without the rep, you can't upgrade your car with the coolest modifications. Without the bank, though, you can't afford to. But building up your rep means you'll get the attention of Palm City's police—and they don't play nice with racers.

The first Need for Speed since 2017's Payback takes us right back to the glory days of the series, mixing the open-world racing challenges of the classic Need for Speed: Most Wanted with the bright lights and rain-slicked city streets of Need for Speed: Underground. It's got a phenomenal list of cars to drive, mixing muscle cars from Dodge, Chevrolet, and Ford with hot hatches from Honda and Volkswagen, plus supercars from Lamborghini and Ferrari. You can trick them all out with new paint jobs, custom decals, spoilers, and more. Can you handle the heat? Well, get out there and drive!

QUICK TIPS:

USE THE HANDBRAKE
■ Slow and steady braking to make it around the corners will slow you down too much. You'll lose. Use the handbrake to drift around the sharper bends, and you have a better chance of winning.

BANK ON YOUR REP
■ Bank and rep are both crucial, so you need to drive day and night. Without building both, you'll lose out on the cars and upgrades you need to win.

CUT CORNERS
■ Don't worry too much about clipping walls or roadside obstacles. They'll slow you down, but won't do much damage. As long as you clear the checkpoints, it doesn't matter if you cut the corners.

FAST AND FURIOUS

SPEEDHUNTERS SHOWDOWN
■ During the day, you can race in the Speedhunters Showdown racing festival, earning bank if you can win its circuit races and challenges.

FAST FACT:
Heat is the 24th game in the Need for Speed series, which has now had more reboots than Batman. In fact, the series contains two remakes: 2010's Hot Pursuit and 2012's Most Wanted.

SMASH THE RECORDS
■ Day and night, you've got extra challenges to pull off and collectibles to find. Smash through billboards, set speed records, and try to meet your day and night challenge objectives.

REP FOR RACING
■ At night, you'll have more races and challenges to boost your rep—and it's after the sun goes down that the game's tale of cops and racers really comes alive.

CRAZY CHASES
■ Win races, complete challenges, and drive around Palm City and you're going to get chased by the police. Escape and make it to a safe house, or get captured and lose your cash!

STORM WARNING
■ Watch out for the weather. Storms and heavy rain make it harder to see the course in front and leave your tires slip-sliding all over the track. Those turns get even more tricky!

IT'S LIKE: FORZA HORIZON 4
■ There's a lot of classic Need for Speed in here, but the racing festival is straight out of the Forza Horizon games—still the best racing games around!

TRY: BURNOUT PARADISE REMASTERED
■ Burnout Paradise is a classic open-world racing game that goes just as big on fast cars and crazy chases. This PS4 and Xbox One remaster shows the gameplay hasn't aged one bit.

TEAM SONIC

RACING

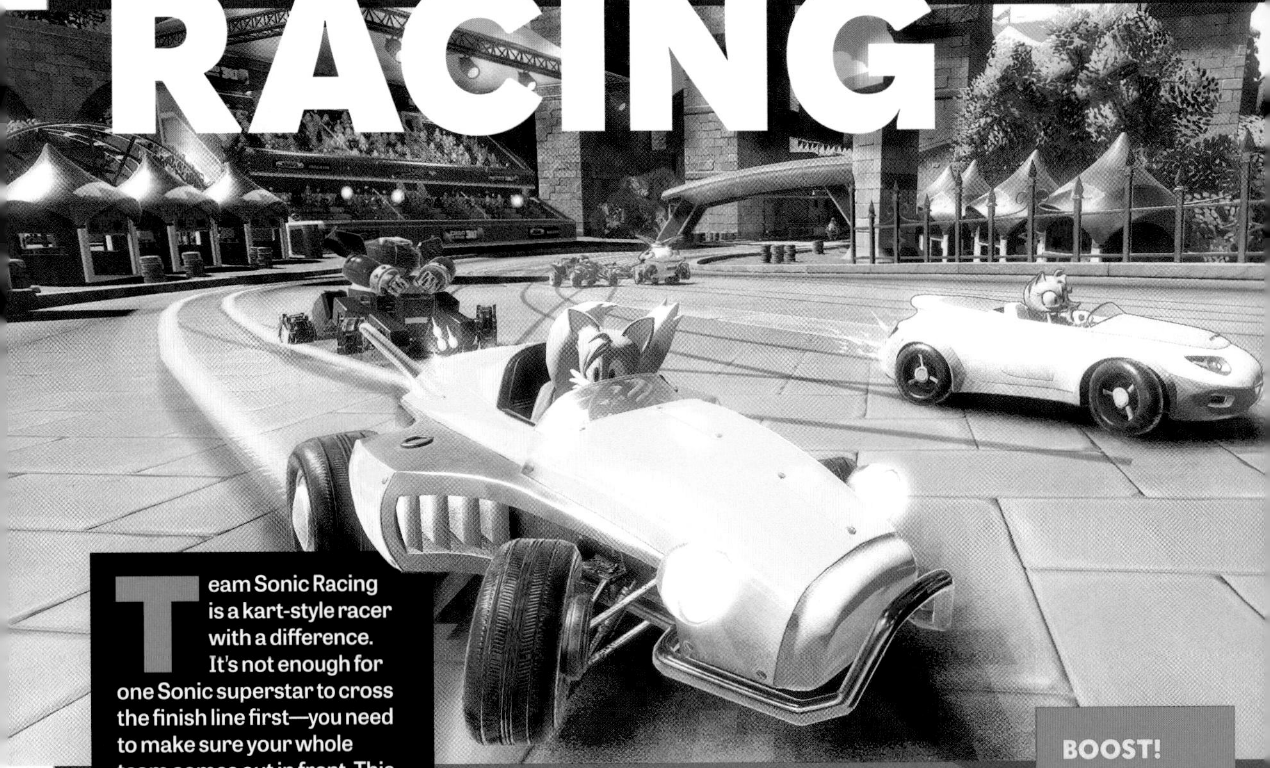

Team Sonic Racing is a kart-style racer with a difference. It's not enough for one Sonic superstar to cross the finish line first—you need to make sure your whole team comes out in front. This means mastering a bunch of team racing techniques, plus a selection of sweet power-ups and some of the most challenging kart courses around!

Sonic, Tails, Amy, and Knuckles all get their turn in the driver's seat, along with other favorites from the spikey blue hero's best games. And while it's the multiplayer action that will keep you coming back, there's a meaty co-op story mode to get through, not to mention time trial challenges and some cool car customization tools. Where other kart racers only want to rip off Mario Kart, this one's packed with fresh ideas—and almost too much Sonic speed to handle!

QUICK TIPS:

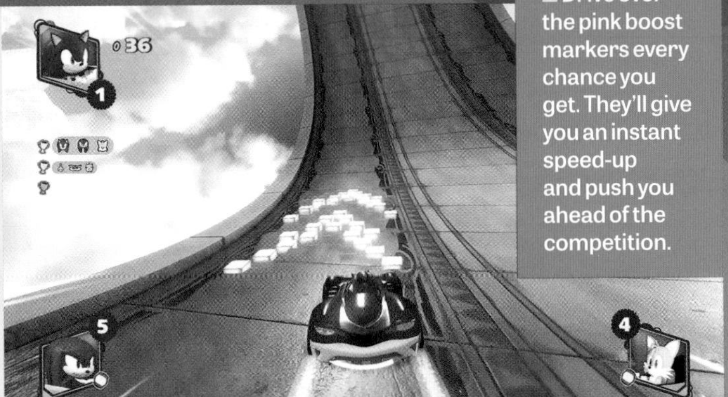

BOOST!
■ Drive over the pink boost markers every chance you get. They'll give you an instant speed-up and push you ahead of the competition.

SHARE THE SPOILS
■ Got a power-up you don't want to use? Tap the B or circle button to find out if someone else on your team can use it. They might have a power-up for you later. If so, tap B to accept it.

TAKE A SHORTCUT
■ There are dozens of different routes you can take through each race. Try taking different directions to see if a shortcut will give you an advantage over the other team.

GO TEAM!

SLINGSHOT
■ Teammates racing ahead of you leave a yellow slipstream behind them. Drive inside it and your car will get a speed boost. You can use it to slingshot in front of your buddy.

SKIM-BOOST
■ See a teammate skidding or struggling because they've been hit by a rocket or obstacle? Speed close by them, and they'll speed up nicely and regain control of their car.

FAST FACT:
Team Sonic Racing features fifteen favorite Sonic heroes and villains divided into different teams. If you don't want to field Sonic, Tails, and Knuckles, how about Metal Sonic, Dr. Eggman, and Shadow?

CUSTOMIZE YOUR RIDE
■ Between races, you can give your car an upgrade. Win and you earn credits to buy mod pods, which give you new parts to boost your speed, acceleration, or handling.

RIVAL TEAM TAKEDOWNS
■ Sometimes the other team doesn't play fair, so why should you? Hit them with power-ups or shunt them off the track, and you'll get a rival team takedown bonus.

ULTIMATE SPEED
■ Keep up the team boosts and takedowns, and you'll charge up your Team Ultimate power. Trigger it to go and get a whopping speed boost. You can make it last longer if two or more of you activate the power at once.

TRY: TRACKMANIA
■ Looking for a crazy racer that breaks all the rules? TrackMania is back as an online racer crammed with loop-the-loop and corkscrew tracks, plus outrageous stunt car challenges.

IT'S LIKE: MARIO KART 8 DELUXE
■ The greatest ever version of the classic kart racer, stuffed with tracks and racers from all seven previous Mario Kart games.

TRAIN TO

Every player has to start somewhere, and not everyone has the raw gaming talent to become a YouTube gaming guru or the next Fortnite champ. Play the best games, though, and build your skills, and you'll be ready to take on the toughest games.

Think of this as a Game On! college course in gaming, running through five sets of gaming challenges that will take you from gaming noob to master level. We don't expect you to finish them all—you'd need every console and it would cost you a fortune—but pick a couple, give them your best shot, and keep taking your skills up to the next level.

EASY LEVEL

TAKE A JOURNEY

■ Journey isn't just one of the best indie games ever—it's also one of the easiest games to complete. The puzzles aren't too tricky, and things that are trying to kill you are few and far between. Just about anyone should be able to get through it in around three hours, yet it's still incredibly satisfying to play. It's a brilliant beginner's game.

COMPLETE A ROBLOX OBBY

■ Roblox obstacle course games, or Obbies, work like pint-sized platform games, and while there are some that will stress your nerves beyond their limits, you can polish off most of the more popular Obbies with just a little skill and patience. Try Escape Grandma's House or The Really Easy Obby. (But not Mega Fun Obby. With over 1,500 levels, it will take you forever!)

GAME

Have you got what it takes to join the gaming greats?

RAISE YOUR GRADE: Complete the game and get a True Believer on every level

BE A TRUE BELIEVER

■ Nearly all the Lego games are ideal noob-fodder. Mix simple puzzles with simple combat and the fact that you can't die, and it's almost impossible to fail. However, each game has a special True achievement in each level for collecting a set amount of Lego studs. Load up Lego Marvel Super Heroes or Lego Marvel Super Heroes 2, and see if you can bag a True Believer.

WINNING TEAM

■ Overwatch is a lot easier on the less-skilled gamer than most FPS games. You can pick up the basics quickly, though the serious skills take years to master. For this challenge, we want you to win a match with a team of friends or random players, but also rack up five eliminations. This doesn't mean you have to get the final blow—just do your part to bring down an enemy.

DEFEAT KING MACFRIGHT

■ Don't be afraid of Luigi's Mansion 3—it's not a difficult game and there's nothing really scary to be frightened of. Some of the bosses might take a couple of tries before you beat them, but with most you just have to figure out their attack patterns, then weaken them enough to suck them up. King MacFright on the sixth floor is the first tricky boss. Can you take him?

NOT THE LAST JEDI

■ Completing Star Wars Jedi: Fallen Order on Jedi Master or Grand Master difficulties is no walk in the park, but on Story Mode? It's easy! Not only will playing the game on the lowest difficulty level make you feel like the toughest Jedi Master since Yoda, but you'll get a great grounding in modern gameplay, and you can switch to a higher level whenever you like!

▶

BATTLE BOWSER

■ We've lost count of how many games there are in which Mario has a boss battle with Bowser, but you can't say you're a gamer until you've knocked the Koopa King off his throne. Play any 2D or 3D Mario game and make it through to the final Bowser battle, then teach Marlo's archenemy a lesson. And, no, mid-game battles where he slips off halfway through don't count. Too easy!

GET A TOP 5 FINISH

■ You won't win a Victory Royale in a Fortnite: Battle Royale match without some serious building and shooting skills, but it's nowhere near as hard to place in the top five. Go sneaky, hide, and pick your fights wisely, and you can easily get through to the final handful. You might even make it without firing a single shot.

RAISE YOUR GRADE: Complete Halo 2 or Halo 3 on Heroic difficulty

SAVE HUMANITY

■ By our count, the Master Chief has saved humanity or the galaxy at least five times, though he doesn't always stop the Covenant or Prometheans for good. In this challenge, just complete any Halo game on the Normal difficulty mode, and prove you're worthy of filling the massive boots of the Master Chief.

ESCAPE THE LAW

■ You can win during the day in Need for Speed Heat, but can you get away from the police at night? Rev your engines and start this challenge by taking first place in any nighttime event, then drive around long enough to get chased by the police. All you need to do is lose the cops and make it to a safe house without getting arrested. Can you escape the law?

DEFEAT ABZU

■ Final Fantasy VII Remake isn't short of tough boss battles—though nothing as bad as the optional Weapon battles we're expecting to see in part two. While some of your enemies are new, Abzu returns from the original version—and he's more of a pain to fight second time around. Trash this big, bad monster and notch up another challenge completed.

ALL 12 CUPS

■ Reckon you've mastered Mario Kart 8 Deluxe? Prove it by winning the top spot on the podium with a gold in all 12 cups. You can use your favorite driver and have whatever vehicle and wheels you want, but you have to win a gold in every cup on the 150cc level or above. Now, that's real racing!

CONTENDER LEVEL

MASTER THE MOUNTAINS

■ Lonely Mountains: Downhill features some of the most fearsome mountain-biking tracks around. It's a true test of speed, determination, and nerves, especially once time limits start creeping in. That's when you need to start ignoring your set paths and take the really tricky shortcuts. Complete the Beginners Challenges on every trail on all four mountains to prove you've got what it takes.

DEFEAT DRACULA

■ Castlevania: Symphony of the Night is an all-time classic and the best Castlevania. It's also the easiest, but with a series this difficult, it's still no cakewalk. If you want to demonstrate your old-school gaming skills, you need to work your way through Dracula's castle and beat the villainous vamp in his lair.

FIGHT FRIEZA

■ There's a whole lot of fighting to be done in Dragon Ball Z: Kakarot, with three massive story arcs to battle your way through. It will take you hours to reach the end of the whole Saiyan saga, but can you make it to the end of the second chapter and defeat the evil emperor, Frieza? Power up your heroes before you try this one—it's hard.

CHAMPION OF GALAR

■ Simply beating all eight gym leaders in Pokémon Sword or Pokémon Shield is tough enough, but can you then go on to complete the game's story, save the world, and defeat the reigning champ? This one's going to demand advanced Pokémon skills and a rock-solid Pokémon lineup. Want to win it? You'll have to bring it!

FIFTY FIGHTERS

■ There are 69 fighters in Super Smash Bros. Ultimate, and that's without all the extra fighters in the two Fighters Passes. All you need to do is unlock 50 by playing through the different game modes, waiting for a challenger match, then beating the challenger whenever one arrives. Prepare for a real battle if you want to get King Dedede or Marth.

REACH THE THRONE ROOM

■ Dead Cells can be a merciless game—just like the Dead Souls games that helped inspire it. For this challenge, we want you to make it through to the final Throne Room battle, but that's going to take a good run through the game without dying, plus some pretty awesome weapons and powers. If you want to survive, you're going to have to get good.

Dead Cells (Alpha Branch) - 4 Cell Difficulty Throne Room Fight.

The Hand of the King

0:22 / 2:29

RAISE YOUR GRADE: Reach the Throne Room and defeat the Hand of the King

RAISE YOUR GRADE: Beat the Darker Side of the Moon without losing a single life

GO TO THE DARKER SIDE

■ There's nothing too vicious in the main Super Mario Odyssey adventure, but keep going and collect those power moons, and you unlock one final adventure. We don't want you to simply reach the Darker Side of the Moon—we want you to beat its challenge and defeat some of your toughest enemies yet. Are you and Mario up to the job?

WIN A VICTORY ROYALE

■ There's only one thing that counts in Fortnite: Battle Royale, and that's bagging a Victory Royale. That means landing with 99 other players and coming out as the last one standing, and that takes skill, strategy, and a certain amount of luck. You can practice in Squads or Duos, but we don't want anyone carrying you. To complete this challenge, win the Victory Royale playing solo.

#1 VICTORY ROYALE

GIANT KILLER

■ Shadow of the Colossus features 16 of the biggest bosses in gaming history, each one a titanic battle worthy of a legend. From the 10th onward, they start getting really tough. You'll face epic journeys and long climbs just to reach them, and you'll have to find ways to slow them down or bring them back to Earth. And then—somehow—you've got to slay them. Getting all 16 is no small challenge.

BEAT KING DICE

■ Cuphead is notoriously difficult. Underneath those lovely 1930s cartoon graphics lies one of the most brutally challenging tests of skill and reflexes ever made. Gamers have spent years debating which of the game's bosses is the worst, but we're putting our money on King Dice. Beat his gauntlet of bosses and you've earned our respect.

SLAY THE ENDER DRAGON

■ Minecraft is one of the most generous and welcoming games around—until you reach its endgame boss, the Ender Dragon. It spawns in the End dimension once you reach it, then proceeds to whack you with fireballs, flame attacks, and charging attacks. To make things worse, it's a massive damage sponge. Hope you brought your best gear. You're going to need it!

FIGHT SHIN AKUMA

■ Simply reaching Street Fighter V's hidden boss is no picnic. You have to complete the arcade mode without losing a round, then defeat the punishingly tough M. Bison. Manage that, and you're up against a monster that hurls fireballs and unblockable attacks like there's no tomorrow. He also puts in a guest appearance in Tekken 7, where he's just as mean. It's all going to end in tears. Yours.

MASTER LEVEL

CLIMB TO THE TOP

■ Don't let its charming story and retro graphics fool you—Celeste is a vicious piece of work. Each bite-sized level is a platform gaming puzzle filled with nasty insta-death traps and near-impossible feats of jumping, and the farther you go up the game's mountain, the nastier and nearer to impossible they become. Make it to the end without any assists? You're a gaming master.

NUZLOCKE RUN

■ We know what you're thinking: surely anyone can complete Pokémon Sword or Pokémon Shield? Well, how about tackling the Nuzlocke challenge? The rules go like this: You can only capture the first Pokémon you meet in each new area, and if a Pokémon faints, it's considered dead and you have to release it. Sounds easy? Try it. You'll be unpleasantly surprised.

LEGENDARY, ALL SKULLS 'ON

■ Completing a Halo game on Normal is no biggie. Finishing it on Heroic only just counts as an achievement. Reaching the credits on Legendary? Now we're talking. But completing a Halo game on Legendary with all the Skull extra challenges turned on? You're either a glutton for punishment with too much time on your hands, or your skills are truly awesome.

COUNT TO 20

■ Apex Legends demands high-level shooting skills and a mastery of the different Legends' abilities, and with a smaller lobby and no equivalent of Tilted Towers, it's rare to see massive kill counts. Only a handful of players have even hit 30. That's why we're challenging you—and not your team—to rack up 20 or more eliminations in a single game, then go on to win the match. What kind of Legend are you?

THE PATH OF PAIN

■ Hollow Knight isn't always as easy as it looks, with some fiendishly difficult platform puzzles and some bosses that seem to have wandered in from a Dark Souls game. Nothing, though, will prepare you for the Path of Pain, a new optional area in the White Palace that's, well, exactly as bad as it sounds. You can beat it, but it might bring tears to your eyes.

RAISE YOUR GRADE: Beat the Path of Pain without using any Soul Totems to recharge your Soul

GROUNDED

CAN YOU SURVIVE IN YOUR OWN BACKYARD?

Did you love the ant-sized antics of Marvel's *Ant-Man*? Have you ever seen '80s classic *Honey, I Shrunk the Kids* and wanted to be one of them? Well, Grounded takes a similar spin on the survival game. Here, a foursome of teens get shrunk to the size of bugs, only for the experimental equipment to fail. Until they can figure out how to return to normal size, they'll have to face the perils of an overgrown backyard.

Angry ants, hostile mites, and predatory spiders all want to get you, and at this scale even shrubs and puddles pose a threat. Luckily, our young heroes are crafty and resourceful—and they won't stay defenseless for long!

■ When you're tiny, insects can be deadly. These bees won't bother you unless you bother them, but what happens if you do?

■ You can't survive the backyard without weapons and armor, but with the right blueprints and the right materials, you can craft your own stuff. Spears and axes can be built from plant stalks and sharp chunks of gravel, while pieces of bark and insect exoskeletons can be bound with grass fibers to make armor.

■ You won't always find what you need above the surface. Sometimes you'll have to investigate tunnels where ants and spiders lurk, or even dive into the depths of flooded areas.

■ Nobody's safe in the wilderness without shelter, but start chopping away at the vegetation and you can get what you need to build walls and put a roof over your head. Before long, you'll have food, water, and everything you need to keep you strong.

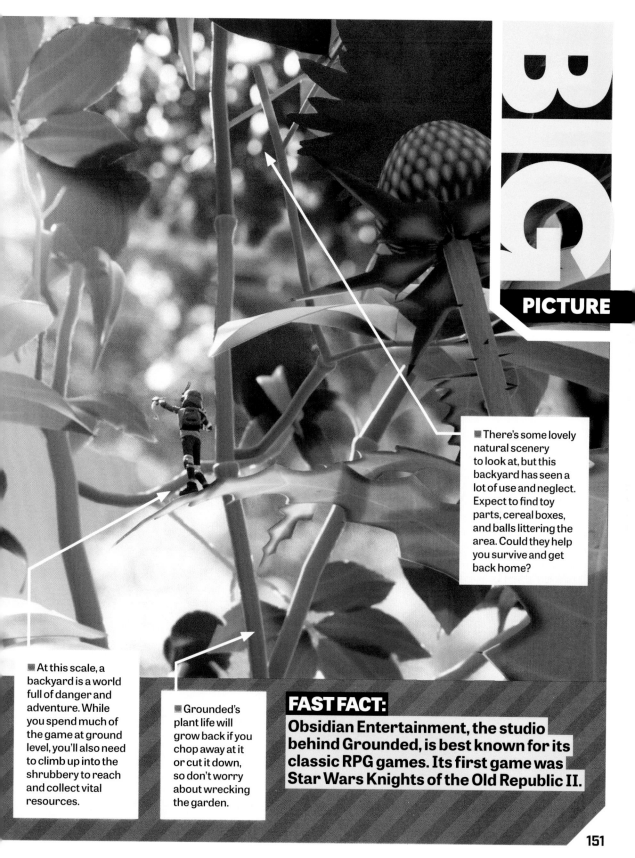

BIG

■ There's some lovely natural scenery to look at, but this backyard has seen a lot of use and neglect. Expect to find toy parts, cereal boxes, and balls littering the area. Could they help you survive and get back home?

■ At this scale, a backyard is a world full of danger and adventure. While you spend much of the game at ground level, you'll also need to climb up into the shrubbery to reach and collect vital resources.

■ Grounded's plant life will grow back if you chop away at it or cut it down, so don't worry about wrecking the garden.

FAST FACT:
Obsidian Entertainment, the studio behind Grounded, is best known for its classic RPG games. Its first game was Star Wars Knights of the Old Republic II.

151

JOURNEY TO THE SAVAGE PLANET

EXPLORE A STRANGE WORLD AND ALIEN CULTURES—AND TRY TO MAKE IT BACK ALIVE

Exploring space is a challenging gig. Kindred Aerospace —the fourth best interstellar exploration company—has dumped you on a distant world crawling with hostile life-forms, your ship is damaged, and you have zero equipment and zero fuel. Forget getting promoted. How will you survive?

In this Journey to the Savage Planet, you'll have to keep your wits about you. Harvested minerals and alien plant extracts can go into your ship's 3D printer, and become new weapons and tools. Keep exploring and scanning the local critters, and you'll find ways to deal with the planet's biggest perils. Most importantly, this world holds the ruins of an alien civilization. What can you learn about them, and what will that knowledge be worth?

QUICK TIPS:

DON'T BE A STRANGER
■ Return to your ship regularly to bank your resources and upgrade your equipment. If you get killed, you'll lose your resources until you grab the resource package from where you died.

KEEP YOUR EYES OPEN
■ The world is full of resources, useful plants, points to grapple from, and obstacles you can blow up. Even if you can't do anything with them now, you might be able to use them later.

IF IT GLOWS, BLAST IT
■ Some creatures are friendly, but others just want you dead. Try blasting any glowing body parts, and look for ways to weaken them or take them by surprise. It's you or them!

SURVIVE THE SAVAGE WORLD

SCAN THE WILDLIFE
■ One of your top jobs as an explorer is to scan everything you can. As a bonus, you'll get tips on using the plants or handling any hostile creatures.

UPGRADE YOUR GEAR
■ Kill the mean critters and destroy certain rocks and plants, and you'll find resources you can use to upgrade your equipment. If you're lucky, Kindred scientists might even help you out with new gear.

WATCH OUT FOR NEW PERILS
■ Danger is everywhere. Predators want to eat you. Tentacled monsters want to kill you. Weird plants send out jets of burning acid goo. You'll be lucky to survive five minutes.

JUMP AND GRAPPLE
■ Two essential early upgrades will give you a rocket-boosted jump and a grapple ability. Use them to reach new areas or make gravity-defying leaps.

DEFEND YOURSELF
■ Keep your pistol handy and blast anything that attacks. It's pretty weak at first, but upgrades will boost the damage, capacity, and more.

CLOSE ENCOUNTERS
■ Look carefully and you'll find fragments of a grand alien civilization. There might even be advanced alien technology that you can use to get around.

FAST FACT:
There's no map in Journey to the Savage Planet. The team at Typhoon Studios wanted you to focus on the exploration and adventure, not checking boxes on a map screen.

IT'S LIKE: METROID PRIME: TRILOGY
■ Nintendo's Wii and GameCube classics had a similar balance of combat and exploration on alien worlds. Come on, Nintendo. Any chance of a Switch remake before the upcoming sequel?

TRY: OUTER WILDS
■ Ready for another weird and wonderful space adventure? Outer Wilds gives you mystery in a distant solar system, where the sun is on the verge of imploding.

WIN IN OVERWATCH AND OVERWATCH 2

Winning in Overwatch and Overwatch 2 isn't about raw shooting skills or mastering abilities—it's about understanding how the game works and changing the way you play it. Most of all, it's about how you work as part of a mighty fighting team. You can get away with being a lone wolf in other shooters, but in Overwatch it's going to get you nowhere!

KNOW YOUR WEAKNESSES

■ Even Overwatch's mightiest heroes have their weaknesses. Reaper is brilliant in a close-up fight, but useless at long range. Widowmaker is a lethal sniper, but vulnerable in the open against tough enemies like Genji or Reinhardt. If you're in a fight you can't win, get out of it. Escape, find some friends, heal up, then jump back into business.

TANK HEROES are designed to form the front line of defense, provide cover for the team, and soak up enemy bullets while the Damage players go in for the kill.

SUPPORT HEROES provide shields, healing, and damage bonuses to the rest.

■ Think about your hero and their role while you're playing, you'll play better for your team. If you start playing Tank heroes like a one-man army, you're not going to help them to the win.

KNOW YOUR ROLE

■ In Overwatch, all the heroes fit into three main roles: Tank, Support, and Damage.

DAMAGE HEROES are designed to push for the objectives, harass the enemy, and notch up eliminations.

MAKE THE MOST OF YOUR ABILITIES

■ Your attack moves are important, but don't forget your other abilities—the ones you activate by pressing L1 or R1 on your controller. They're really important but tend to have short cooldown times, which means you can keep on using them in a match.

■ Your Ultimate is different, because it takes so long to charge up. Rather than waste it on a quick kill, use it where it's going to make a difference. Even better, keep an eye on your teammates and see if you can all use your abilities at the same time. It could turn the whole direction of a match!

LISTEN UP!

■ You can learn a lot in Overwatch just by listening. Different characters have different footsteps, and those of your teammates will usually be quieter than the footsteps of the enemy team. Each hero also makes a different sound or speech when they unleash their Ultimate, and these actually change if that hero is on the other team!

MIX THINGS UP

■ Do you keep getting stomped by the same enemies in the same area? Don't keep coming back for more. Switch characters and find a hero who can make a difference. You might be able to counter your enemies or help your team push forward. And don't keep attacking from the same direction. Take a route around the side and surprise the enemy team, or use abilities to hit them from a different angle. Most of all, work with your teammates. If you rush in one by one, you're only going to get hurt.

FAST FACT:
Overwatch hero Zarya is based on a real-life person—a Blizzard employee who worked as a character designer on the game.

COUNTER

■ The real trick to Overwatch is learning to counter enemy abilities, so that if the other team is blocking with Bastion or chalking up cheap hook-and-blast kills with Roadhog, you can do something to stop them. For instance, Genji's Deflection ability is brilliant for shielding from frontal attacks and getting in close, while Reinhardt and Roadhog are great for pinning down tough characters who can do a lot of damage. There's loads of advice about this online, so go and do some research.

FINAL FANTASY VII REMAKE

Things have changed in the last 23 years of gaming, and this year's remake of the classic Final Fantasy VII shows by just how much. This isn't your average visual update with slick, new HD graphics, but a whole new game, based on the original, that brings this vintage masterpiece into the modern age.

The team at Square Enix has rebuilt all the characters for modern consoles. With realistic costumes and lifelike skin and hair, they're worlds apart from the original stars, but they still have the styles and personalities that older fans will know and love.

FAST FACT:
Cloud and FFVII's other biggest stars have been redesigned by Tetsuya Nomura, who created them for the original. Nomura has worked on every Final Fantasy from FFVI to FFXV except for Final Fantasy IX.

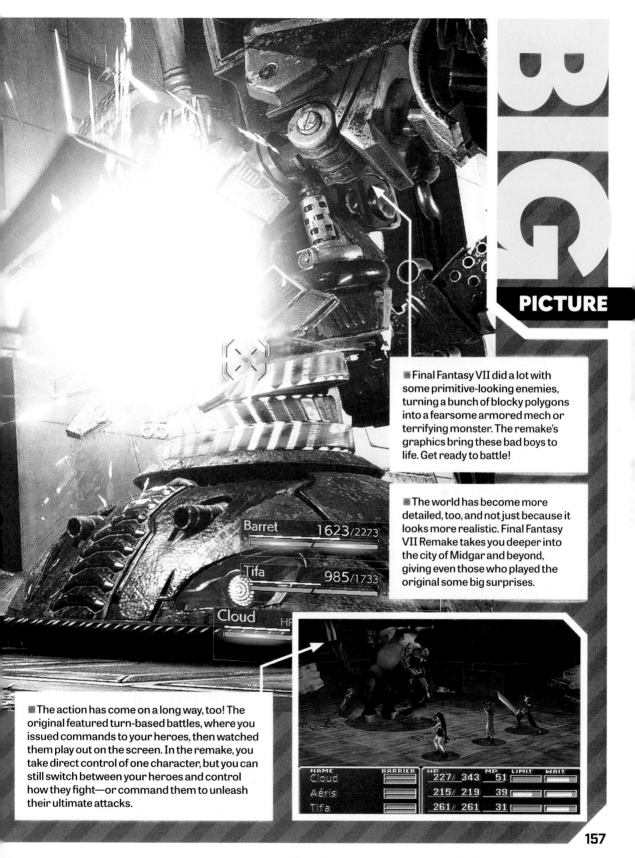

Final Fantasy VII did a lot with some primitive-looking enemies, turning a bunch of blocky polygons into a fearsome armored mech or terrifying monster. The remake's graphics bring these bad boys to life. Get ready to battle!

The world has become more detailed, too, and not just because it looks more realistic. Final Fantasy VII Remake takes you deeper into the city of Midgar and beyond, giving even those who played the original some big surprises.

The action has come on a long way, too! The original featured turn-based battles, where you issued commands to your heroes, then watched them play out on the screen. In the remake, you take direct control of one character, but you can still switch between your heroes and control how they fight—or command them to unleash their ultimate attacks.

Barret 1623/2273

Tifa 985/1733

Cloud HP

NAME	BARRIER	HP	MP	LIMIT	WAIT
Cloud		227// 343	51		
Aéris		215// 219	39		
Tifa		261// 261	31		

157

THE VILLAINS
OF THE LEGEND OF ZELDA

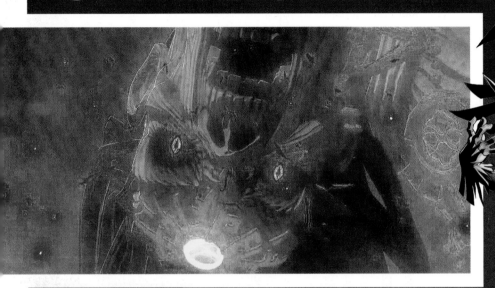

With the sequel to The Legend of Zelda: Breath of the Wild around the corner, we're all excited to discover what peril now faces the kingdom of Hyrule.

All we've seen so far is an ancient, mummified form brought back to life by some mysterious enchantment—and awaken with hatred in its eyes. Has a new form of Ganon returned to wreak havoc on the realm, or will Link and Zelda be going up against a new threat? Is this, as some say, an old villain brought back from the dead, or a legendary hero corrupted by dark forces?

While Link has only ever had one archenemy, he's taken on other adversaries—and defeated them all!

GANON/GANONDORF
■ Ganon started out as a purple, pig-like demon, but by The Legend of Zelda: Ocarina of Time he'd morphed into the Gerudo sorcerer, Ganondorf. Ganondorf was responsible for transforming Hyrule into a land of darkness in the Nintendo 64 classic, then reappearing in both The Wind Waker and Twilight Princess to menace the kingdom. When the power of the Triforce is at stake, we wouldn't be surprised to see Link's nemesis return once more.

MAJORA
■ An evil spirit inhabiting a cursed mask doesn't sound like a terrifying villain, but Majora made The Legend of Zelda: Majora's Mask one of the darkest and creepiest of Zelda games. Its true form is never seen, but it possesses its poor puppet, the Skull Kid, and through him tries to bring doom to the land of Termina.

DEMISE

■ The villain of Legend of Zelda: Skyward Sword is even bigger and scarier than Ganondorf! Demise is the demon king of ancient Hyrule, defeated thousands of years before by the goddess, Hylia, but reborn during the events of Skyward Sword. Even after being defeated by Link, he boasts that he'll be back in another form to destroy Hyrule and its defenders in a future time. Does he mean Ganondorf? The top Zelda scholars think so!

YUGA

■ The big bad of The Legend of Zelda: A Link Between Worlds is an evil sorcerer with the power to transform himself and others into painted art. He's on a mission to find and imprison the seven sages that protect the kingdom of Hyrule—and if he can get Link and Zelda along the way, that's just a bonus! Of course, Yuga might not be working on his own…

FAST FACT:

The Zelda timeline can be confusing. Breath of the Wild is set thousands of years later than its predecessor, Skyward Sword, as they're chronologically Link's first and last adventures.

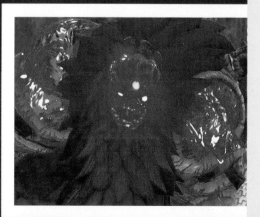

CALAMITY GANON

■ Calamity Ganon is an ancient evil that emerges from beneath Hyrule Castle 100 years before Link awakens in The Legend of Zelda: Breath of the Wild. Trapped by Princess Zelda in the castle, it's still able to send its dark magic—the Malice—out to rampage through Hyrule, while its four Scourges infect the Divine Beasts that were created to protect the kingdom. When Link finally meets Calamity Ganon, it's clear that it's an incomplete form of Ganon—and if that's so, we're not looking forward to crossing swords with the real deal!

TALES OF ARISE

THE EPIC RPG SERIES IS BACK WITH THE BEST TALES YET!

For millions of years, the planets Dahna and Rena have stuck together in close orbit. The people of Dahna worship Rena, believing it's a paradise planet of the gods. Yet for over 300 years, the people of Rena have secretly enslaved them, robbing the people of Dahna of their history, their freedom, and even their lives! Now a clash brings the two planets together. Alphen is a young Dahnan man with no memory and no sense of pain. Shionne is a young Renan woman with a terrible curse. What happens when the two combine with a flaming sword and a tale of adventure?

Japanese RPG fans have always loved the Tales series, but it's never been as big as Final Fantasy here in the West. Tales of Arise deserves to change that. It's a stunning-looking game set across two stunning-looking fantasy worlds, with huge areas to explore, powerful foes to battle, and magic and mysteries to discover. It's also action-packed with a brilliant storyline, so prepare to settle in for a few weeks—or even several months!

QUICK TIPS:

LEARN YOUR COMBOS
■ When you're fighting, Tales of Arise is more like a fighting game than your typical RPG, so make sure you know how to string your attacks and magic "Artes" together to maximize the damage.

GO AUTO
■ If you find the combat too challenging, you can switch from Manual to Semi-Auto or Auto battle modes. In Semi-Auto, your console takes care of movement automatically, while in Auto it basically fights for you unless you pause it and give it new commands.

GET OUT AND EXPLORE
■ While it's not an open world game, there's a lot to do and see in Tales of Arise. Search for treasure and take on some side quests. Talk to everyone you meet. You never know how something you find now might help you later on in the tale!

A TALE OF TWO WORLDS

THE BROODING HERO
■ Alphen is the central hero of Tales of Arise. With his face half-covered by a shattered mask, he has no memory and no sense of pain—handy when there's a burning hot magic sword around!

WARRIOR FROM ANOTHER WORLD
■ Shionne is a Renan warrior who learns the truth about her planet and what it's doing to Dahna. She's cursed to cause pain to everyone she touches. Will she betray her people and join Alphen in his quest?

FAST FACT:

The Tales series is now 25 years old, with Tales of Phantasia making its debut on the Super NES back in 1995. There have been 19 Tales in the series so far.

A TRAPPED PLANET
■ While the world of Rena has advanced technology and magic, the world of Dahna is stuck in the medieval era and crawling with dangerous monsters. Prepare to fight!

ROAM THE WILDERNESS
■ While you can't explore the whole of Dahna or Rena, there are some huge areas of wilderness to investigate. Who knows what ancient ruins and magic objects you'll discover if you look around?

TAKE CONTROL
■ Tales of Arise has an action-heavy take on RPG combat, where you're in control. Move around your enemies, then rush in with killer combos— and remember to use your magic Artes.

IT'S LIKE: DRAGON QUEST XI: ECHOES OF AN ELUSIVE AGE
■ Dragon Quest XI is a more traditional RPG than Tales of Arise, but it has a similar sense of epic exploration, strong characters, and a great story.

TRY: FINAL FANTASY CRYSTAL CHRONICLES REMASTERED
■ An exclusive for the old Nintendo GameCube, this lovable Final Fantasy offshoot now has a second chance to shine, with versions for Switch, PS4, and smartphones, plus a brilliant multiplayer mode.

STORY OF SEASONS

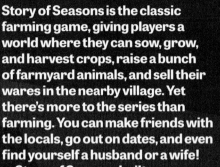

Story of Seasons is the classic farming game, giving players a world where they can sow, grow, and harvest crops, raise a bunch of farmyard animals, and sell their wares in the nearby village. Yet there's more to the series than farming. You can make friends with the locals, go out on dates, and even find yourself a husband or a wife!

Story of Seasons built up an enthusiastic fanbase, but some of them wanted even more. So, the same team created Rune Factory, which shifted all the farming and romance action of Story of Seasons to a fantasy world. In Rune Factory, you're not just growing crops and raising animals, but exploring dungeons and fighting monsters, too. There's nothing like some loot to upgrade your farm.

Sounds great? It is—and you can now try both of these classic series on Nintendo Switch!

STORY OF SEASONS: FRIENDS OF MINERAL TOWN

■ A remake of one of the most-loved Story of Seasons games, Friends of Mineral Town has all the fun farming action that made the series such a hit. One minute, you'll be busy tending your crops or feeding the sheep and cattle, the next you could be running errands for the kooky villagers and sizing up the local bachelors or bachelorettes.

■ Along the way, there's time for a little horse racing or fishing, while who knows what kind of magical tools you might find underground? You'll even get your own dog and horse to keep you company, though you'll need to take good care of them.

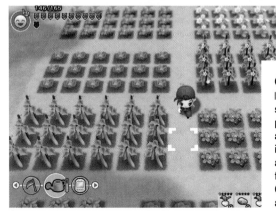

GET FARMING

■ Start off by growing simple crops like sweet potatoes. They're cheap and they grow fast. Corn is also a useful early crop, as you can sell it or use it to feed your chickens. Chickens are the first animal worth buying, and their eggs can help you bring in some extra money.

■ Looking for some easy bonus cash or items? Play the Harvest Goddess mini-game on your TV. Or enter the horse racing festival when the chance comes up.

& RUNE FACTORY

RUNE FACTORY 4 SPECIAL

■ Rune Factory 4 Special is a brilliant Switch update of the last Rune Factory game for the Nintendo 3DS. You still need to succeed as a farmer, growing your vegetables and taking them to market. The difference is that you also need to get out there and be a fantasy hero, fighting through the dungeons, battling monsters, and bringing home the loot.

■ This isn't your usual dungeons and dragons effort. Monsters can be tamed with the right food or gifts, and they'll then join you on your quests, give you goods like milk or wool, or even act as mounts.

■ As in any great RPG, the experience you earn will make you more powerful, while the loot will buy you upgrades to your house and farm. And perhaps your skills as a mighty warrior will go down well with potential dates. Who knows?

FAST FACT:
While the series has always been known as Story of Seasons in Japan, it was called Harvest Moon in North America and Europe. Now the original series continues as Story of Seasons, while a new team makes Harvest Moon games. Confused? Us, too!

Forte

I will do whatever I can to help.

GET FARMING

■ Get your farm going before you start delving into dungeons. Turnips are easy and you'll quickly earn some cash. Once you've got some turnips growing, head to the notice board outside the palace and take on some starter quests. You'll unlock some useful items that will help you.

■ Remember to make friends. The locals are full of hints and tips, and might even join your dungeon-delving party. At the right time, a quick chat could open up a whole new mission. Even the monsters are worth befriending—some tame ones will help you work the farm.

GODS & MONSTERS

USE THE POWERS OF OLYMPUS TO DEFEND THE GODS

With Gods & Monsters, the team behind Assassin's Creed Odyssey are back with a different take on Ancient Greece. This is the Greece of myth and legend, where your mysterious hero must battle a monstrous invasion that threatens the gods of Olympus themselves. Armed with the powers of the gods, it's up to you to fight them off, even if that means going up against their leader, Typhon—the most powerful and deadly monster in Greek myth!

■ Gods & Monsters grew out of the team's research for Assassin's Creed Odyssey, which made them want to revisit the ancient Greek world and explore its mythology, rather than the history. "The stories of the gods and their misadventures have existed through generations of storytellers and audiences, and have transformed into the myths we still know and love today," says the game's producer, Marc-Alexis Côté. "With Gods & Monsters, those tales take on a life of their own, to become a reality to be explored like never before."

■ The Gorgon is another classic Greek monster. As if their snake hair wasn't scary enough, their gaze could turn a man to stone! You'll be fighting these, the many-headed serpent monster, Hydra, and the evil one-eyed giant, Cyclops—and many more legendary enemies—on your quest.

FAST FACT:

In the original Greek myths, Typhon challenges Zeus for the rule of the universe. Zeus was said to have defeated him and thrown him into the fiery prison of Tartarus for eternity.

■ A monstrous hybrid of bird and human, Harpies turn up time and time again in the Greek legends, appearing in the tale of Jason and the Argonauts and attacking the Trojans in Virgil's epic poem, the *Aeneid*. With their giant wings and vicious talons, they're a dangerous threat.

■ One young hero against all of Typhon's fiends—what hope have you got? Plenty. The gods have lent you their powers, so you can journey through the game's epic world and defeat the toughest, whether they're on the ground or in the air.

■ While the team worked to give Assassin's Creed Odyssey a more realistic look, Gods & Monsters is meant to look like a painted world come to life, with beautiful, sunlit landscapes littered with temples, palaces, and statues of the gods. This artistic style puts Gods & Monsters closer to The Legend of Zelda: Breath of the Wild than the Assassin's Creed games.

165

POKÉMON MYSTERY DUNGEON: RESCUE TEAM DX

PIKACHU, MEOWTH, AND SQUIRTLE TO THE RESCUE!

Monty

We came to rescue you.

What would happen if you went to sleep one night and woke up as a Pokémon? Which Pokémon would you become? Which Pokémon would you team up with? Could you join a Pokémon rescue team and go out to help trapped or troubled critters? All these questions—and more—are answered in Pokémon Mystery Dungeon: Rescue Team DX.

A remake of the 2005 Red and Blue Rescue Team games, Pokémon Mystery Dungeon: Rescue Team DX is a Pokémon RPG with a difference. Out goes all the catching and Pokémon battles, in comes dungeons to explore, crazed wild Pokémon to fight, and poor, lost Pokémon in need of rescue. The graphics have been updated with a sweet, hand-painted look, and while the gameplay has dated, it hasn't lost its charm.

QUICK TIPS:

RESCUE MISSIONS
■ Some rescue missions will be delivered to your mailbox, while you'll pick up others from the Post Office bulletin board. It's worth taking on several at once, as you can usually polish off one or two in a single dungeon.

DON'T STARVE
■ It seems Pokémon can't go for longer than a few minutes without a snack! Once your food meter empties, you'll start losing health, so keep it topped up with an apple or a bigger meal.

BE READY TO FIGHT
■ Fighting takes some getting used to, as it doesn't work like it does in other Pokémon games. You attack enemy Pokémon by tapping the A button, but you can also hold down ZL to pick different moves.

IT'S A POKÉMON WORLD!

BECOME A POKÉMON
■ There are no sprawling human cities, gyms, and trainers here. This game's all about the Pokémon and their own world.

HIT THE TOWN
■ The town acts as a hub, linking your rescue HQ and the dungeons with all the shops and training facilities you'll need. You can also pick up gossip in the town square.

Lombre

I don't know why, but there've been many natural disasters lately.

RESCUE HQ
■ Here, you and your teammates relax between missions and get some much-needed sleep. You'll also get missions in your mailbox—and deal with the odd surprise caller!

DUNGEONS
■ Each of the 14 dungeons has its own style, plus several floors of caverns, rooms, and tunnels. You'll have to venture in to find trapped or captured Pokémon—and get them back home.

Monty

Hunh?! Oh no!

FAST FACT:
As in the original, you can't choose which Pokémon you play. Instead, the game runs a personality test to decide the Pokémon that's most like you!

KECLEON STORE
■ Buy supplies for your dungeon adventures and sell the stuff you find with the lizard Pokémon siblings at this store.

Monty

That's the Kecleon Shop.

DOJO
■ You can level up the members of your Pokémon team at the dojo near town. You gain experience faster here than in the dungeons, but you'll need tickets to train and learn new combat moves.

TRY: MOONLIGHTER
■ This one's another action RPG with a difference. Go on dungeon crawling missions to grab stock for your fantasy shop, then build a business selling them to the local heroes.

Sell

IT'S LIKE: POKÉMON SWORD AND SHIELD
■ If you have a Switch and love Pokémon, you need to own one of Pokémon Sword and Shield.

TOP 10

LOOKING FOR FORTNITE FUN? DON'T MISS OUT ON THESE AMAZING MAPS!

CREATIVE MODE MAPS

1

TEAM CRE8
THE FOURTH DIMENSION
■ This isn't just another map, but a full-scale Fortnite adventure, with six themed levels extending from a central hub. Tough platforming and smart puzzles make this an epic map every fan should try.

ISLAND CODE: 1500-2565-8566

HOOSHEN
HOO BALLER PINBALL
■ Fortnite meets Pinball in one awesome multiplayer map. Get inside a Baller and launch onto the table, using the bumpers, chutes, and flippers to score the most points. Can you find all the secret chutes?

ISLAND CODE: 7164-9264-6925

2

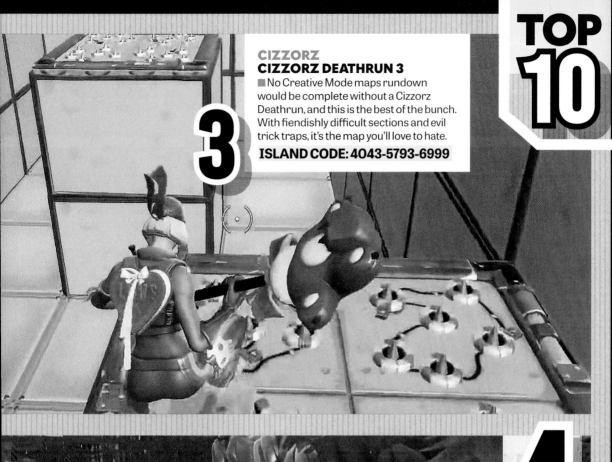

CIZZORZ
CIZZORZ DEATHRUN 3

■ No Creative Mode maps rundown would be complete without a Cizzorz Deathrun, and this is the best of the bunch. With fiendishly difficult sections and evil trick traps, it's the map you'll love to hate.

ISLAND CODE: 4043-5793-6999

3

4

AXEL CAPEK
DURR'S HAUNTED CIRCUIT

■ Having come up with the classic Fury Racing: Snow Summit, Axel Capek knows how to build a racing map. This creepy course could have come straight from Mario Kart. Watch for the spooky shortcuts!

ISLAND CODE: 4837-9287-6622

JESGRAN RUG RIDER
■ Tough maps full of traps are nothing new, but in this one you ride a flying carpet! It's a good-looking map, too, packed with weird scenery to float under and over.

ISLAND CODE: 2778-8561-9992

5

TEAM EVOLVE
SKY STATION SHOWDOWN
■ Get ready to fight! A classic control zone map, where you fight to capture and defend the zones, and rack up more points than the other team. This one gets bonus points for its spectacular sci-fi style.

ISLAND CODE: 2535-1148-3971

6

PRUDIZ
MONSTER ATTACK
■ Prudiz is one of Creative Mode's greatest artists, and this monster vs. starship sculpture could be his best work. Dive in, fly around, and check out the detail in this hand-built creature and the world below.

ISLAND CODE: 2644-1650-6876

7

8

MUSTARD PLAYS
TOMATO HEAD DEATHRUN
■ Creator Mustard Plays claims that over 10,000 Tomato Heads went into the creation of this crazy deathrun—and we believe it! Make the jumps and dodge the death traps on your way to tackle the Tomato King.

ISLAND CODE: 0655-1466-3047

VERITY
SUBWAY SLIDER
■ Inspired by the game Subway Surfer, this map has you sliding along the tracks and the tops of train cars, collecting coins and dodging every obstacle that comes your way. Can you bag the best score?

**ISLAND CODE:
8860-9898-3681**

9

10

SINATIKS
CAMP COAL
■ Prop Hunt maps are always fun, with one player hunting while the others morph into everyday objects. This jungle-themed map is a brilliant piece of work, crammed with ingenious hiding places.

**ISLAND CODE:
0058-2532-2131**

EVERWILD

FANTASTIC BEASTS AND WHERE TO FIND THEM

There's no question that Everwild is one of the most-anticipated Xbox titles out there. Rare—the legendary developers behind Sea of Thieves—have promised a unique and unforgettable adventure based in a natural and magical world. It's one that promises exploration over rugged swamps and mighty forests, where you'll interact with strange, fantastic creatures that behave like real-world animals. Is this Rare's answer to The Legend of Zelda: Breath of the Wild or something even more?

■ Most of Everwild's creatures won't attack you unless they feel threatened, but that doesn't mean you shouldn't be careful. Big cats live inside the caves and come out to hunt. You don't want to provoke them!

ECOSYSTEMS

■ The world has its own ecosystems, where herds of different creatures run together, mothers look after their young, and predators are on the prowl. In a way, it's like a fantasy adventure version of a program on National Geographic or the Discovery Channel. You're going to get up close with some unusual and magical beasts.

FAST FACT:

Rare's game of the Bond movie, *GoldenEye*, was a classic early multiplayer shooter. The mode wasn't part of the original game design and was only added in at the last minute!

■ Exploration plays a big part in the game. You'll need to run, jump, and climb to get where you want to go, and also use stealth to sneak past potentially hostile critters. In these wild landscapes, you'll be stepping far away from the safe, beaten track.

■ Like Sea of Thieves, Everwild is designed as a co-op game, where you share your experience of the wild world and its animals with friends.

BIG

PICTURE

THE RARE LEGACY

■ Rare has been around since the dawn of gaming. As "Ultimate Play the Game," it created early classics like Knight Lore and Underwurlde for the ZX Spectrum and Commodore 64. Then, as Rare, it developed some of the best games for Nintendo consoles, including Battletoads, GoldenEye, and Banjo-Kazooie. More recently, it produced the Kinect Sports games and the awesome Sea of Thieves. You can play many of these games on Xbox One, and there's a brand-new remake of the brilliant Battletoads.

TEMTEM

QUICK TIPS:

HEALING TEMTEM
■ Your Temtem will take a lot of damage in battle, and you need to heal them up between fights. You can use the Temporiums in towns, but keep some Balm and Apples handy while you're roaming around.

WATCH YOUR STAMINA
■ Stamina is a big issue in Temtem. Every move you make drains stamina from a Temtem, and when it's gone they'll get knocked out! Get around this by cycling through your Temtem and resting them in battle.

QUEST REWARDS
■ There's more than one way to collect Temtem. As well as hunting them, you can earn them by completing quests. Finish off some quests and you may get a Temtem reward.

I n its first year, Temtem is already a monster-catching sensation! While it's still a PC-only, early-access release, the team at Crema expect the full game to hit both PC and consoles early on in 2021. It's already a very polished and enjoyable take on the Pokémon style, where you explore the islands of the Airborne Archipelago, battling and taming the various crazy critters, then training them up into a fierce fighting force.

The big difference with Temtem is that you can do it all online, playing co-op through the story with another trainer and joining them in battles. It works with friends and strangers, and you can trade Temtem and provisions. If you're the more experienced trainer,

you can help your friends level up!

The team has big plans for the future, with more islands, more Temtem, more game modes, and even a Fortnite-style Battle Pass. It's a bit like a Pokémon, where the fun never ends!

TAME TO WIN!

PICK YOUR FIRST TEMTEM
■ Once you've designed and named your character, you'll need to choose your first Temtem buddy. You get a choice of three, each with their own strengths and weaknesses. Don't worry if your first Temtem seems puny—you'll get a second, stronger Temtem early on.

Prof. Konstantinos

That Smazee is a 💥 Melee Temtem. It is strong against ✦ Earth and ✦ Crystal, but weak against ✦ Mental. I won it in a pub brawl once in Lochburg. Heady days...

Kenoki

climp

YOU'RE NOT ALONE
■ Temtem looks and plays a lot like Pokémon, but you'll see that there are other players in the game. You don't have to have anything to do with other players if you don't want to, but you can team up with them and play through the story co-op—or challenge them to a Temtem duel.

WILD BATTLES
■ Roam around areas of long grass and it won't be long before you're attacked by wild Temtem. Beat them, play your Temtem card, and you can recruit them for your Temtem team. You only have six slots to work with, but you can swap Temtem in and out at your nearest Temporium.

RIVAL TRAINERS
■ Everywhere you go, you'll meet other tamers. Some will have useful advice on training and battling your own Temtem, while others are just spoiling for a fight! Either way, it's worth fighting just to level up your team and earn some cash.

LEVEL UP
■ With every fight, you'll earn experience, and with time your Temtem will level up and learn new abilities. Some will even evolve into more powerful new forms! Try to cycle through your Temtem while you're in a battle, as only the Temtem that take part will earn experience points.

FAST FACT:
Over half a million people bought and played Temtem in its first month of release, and nearly 400,000 of them lost the tricky first battle against the rival trainer, Max.

IT'S LIKE: POKÉMON SWORD AND SHIELD
■ Play both Pokémon Sword or Shield then Temtem, and it's going to feel pretty familiar, but Temtem does have some cool new twists all of its own.

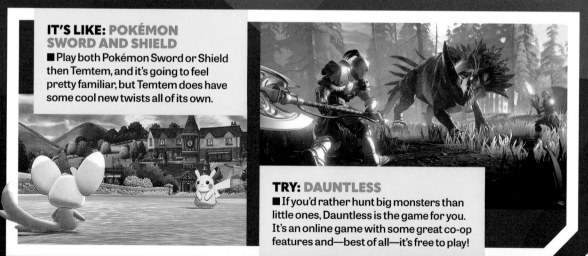

TRY: DAUNTLESS
■ If you'd rather hunt big monsters than little ones, Dauntless is the game for you. It's an online game with some great co-op features and—best of all—it's free to play!

PLANET ZOO

GO WILD WITH THE WILDLIFE AND BUILD A BETTER ZOO

Planet Zoo is the most amazing, in-depth zoo management game that we've ever played. Here, you can build, manage, and enjoy your very own zoo or wildlife park, bringing in all your favorite animals and making sure they get the right environment to thrive. While you're doing that, you have to keep on pleasing your visitors and selling them merchandise and snacks—tiger food costs money, you know—but in this game a zoo is more than just a theme park with wildlife attractions. You're also here to conserve endangered species and return them to the wild, all while balancing the books.

Sound complicated? Well it is, but that doesn't mean it's not a lot of fun. And when you find time to take a break from building habitats and managing a growing team, you can check out your animal population. Chill out with elephants, watch the chimps swing around, or give the wolves a toy to play with. If you like animals (and who doesn't?), you'll love Planet Zoo.

QUICK TIPS:

START WITH CAREER MODE
■ The career mode is fun and challenging, and it also introduces you to all the basics of building and managing a zoo. Don't skip it if you want to get ahead.

UNDERSTAND YOUR GUESTS
■ No, not the visitors, but the animals you're looking after. From the vegetation they like to food, temperature, shelter, and activities, each one has its own needs.

PAY WITH CASH
■ You can buy animals using either cash or conservation credits, but don't waste the credits early on. You're going to need them later for the bigger and more demanding animals.

CONSERVE AND PROTECT

YOUR MISSION

■ Zoos aren't just about making money and keeping the visitors entertained. You also need to educate your public, and conserve and breed endangered species. You can trade them with other zoos or return them to the wild, but you'll need to look after them first.

HAPPY HABITATS

■ Every animal has different needs, and it's easy to forget something important, like a water purifier for the crocodile enclosure or somewhere for the shy springboks and anxious aardvarks to hide. Get it wrong and your animals get sick—and pretty soon the protesters turn up!

PLEASE GIVE GENEROUSLY

■ Keep your animals happy and put up displays to inform your visitors. The more they like the zoo and what you're doing, the more money they'll donate. Selling tickets and drinks will cover your costs, but you'll need more money to build a better zoo and bring in new animals.

BEST BUDDIES

■ Most animals like the company of their own species, but some also get bonuses by having other species in the same enclosure. The ostrich, for example, loves to share space with zebras, warthogs, or giraffes.

RAISE SOME BABIES

■ Get the right males and females together and you could find some new faces in the enclosure. Be careful, though. While some animals make great parents, others can clash with their offspring.

FAST FACT:

This isn't Frontier Developments' first brush with furry critters. The studio also created Zoo Tycoon and Kinectimals for the Xbox and Xbox One.

IT'S LIKE: PLANET COASTER

■ Before Planet Zoo came Planet Coaster, a modern update of the classic Theme Park and RollerCoaster Tycoon games. If you like designing rides and decorating theme parks, dive on in.

TRY: JURASSIC WORLD EVOLUTION

■ The same team also produced this top movie tie-in, which has a lot in common with Planet Zoo. The big difference? If these animals escape, your visitors are twice as likely to get eaten!

ANIMAL CROSSING: NEW HORIZONS

START YOUR NEW LIFE ON A DESERTED ISLAND PARADISE

Don't you sometimes want to get away from it all? Would you like to leave your schoolwork and chores behind to go and relax, hit the beach, feel the sand between your toes or go camping? With Animal Crossing: New Horizons that's the whole idea.

You see, being the biggest name in small-town business is no longer enough for Animal Crossing's bigwig, Tom Nook. He's moving out into the global travel and lifestyle markets, selling package deals to a faraway island, where you can pitch your tent, make some friends, and start a new community. With time, a bunch of tents and basic resources might even transform into a town, but there's plenty of fishing, fruit collecting, bug hunting, crafting, and construction to be getting on with in the meantime. It all adds up to the best and biggest Animal Crossing yet, with an island location so appealing that you might wish you were living there for real!

QUICK TIPS:

WHEN BUGS ATTACK
■ Watch out for dangerous creatures. Spiders, scorpions, and bees can all bite or sting you and leave you feeling really sick.

Ow! Ow ow ow... I got stung by wasps!

TAKE YOUR MEDICINE
■ If you do get stung or bitten, head quickly for Resident Services and buy some medicine. Better still, get some just in case you're attacked.

PULL OUT YOUR PHONE
■ Not sure what to do next? Take a look at your NookPhone. Does someone need a favor or is there an easy way to bring in some Nook Miles?

YOUR NEW ISLAND HOME

CHOOSE YOUR LOOK
■ Create your character and tweak their clothes and hair, then you're ready to depart for your new home. Don't worry if you're not sure about your style—you can change your whole look later.

MAKE SOME FRIENDS
■ You won't be alone on the island. You begin the game with two fellow islanders, both looking forward to starting a new life.

FAST FACT:
Tom Nook is what the Japanese call a tanuki, or a raccoon dog. In Japanese folklore, tanukis are believed to be able to transform leaves into money. This explains the Nook Inc. logo, and if anyone can turn leaves into cash, it's Nook!

ALL THE ESSENTIALS
■ Nook's package gives you all the basics you'll need for island living, including a tent, a lamp, a sleeping bag, and your brand-new NookPhone. The NookPhone comes packed with useful apps.

SET UP CAMP
■ Once you've landed, you need to find a spot to pitch your tent—and two more spots for your new friends to pitch theirs. Make sure you spread out and leave plenty of space.

STORES AND MORE
■ Nook's Resident Services tent is open 24 hours a day and stocks all the stuff you'll need for a simple life. They'll also purchase your unwanted items, so bag yourself some Bells!

flimsy net neous

275

200   200   800   400

360   360   360   640

Timmy

Here's what we have on offer today.

■ The trick is to collect DIY recipes. You can learn them from the workshop at Resident Services and build them on the workbench—or even build your own workbench and make things closer to home.

■ Later on you can customize your furniture and other household items. You can pick different materials and colors, or give your cushions and bedding cool, custom patterns.

Should I craft something using Tom Nook's workbench?

HIT THE WORKBENCH

■ There aren't any stores selling furniture or homeware on the island, at least when you start. If you need something, you're going to have to make it yourself!

■ Find a recipe and all the materials you need, and you can make everything from better tools to a stronger fishing rod to furniture or your own pizza oven—there's no fast food out here!

Everything

Flimsy axe

1.0 × 1.0   Pockets: 0

tree branch ---------- 0 / 5

stone ---------- 0 / 1

Y Sort   X Favorite   B Close

NOOK MILES

■ While you can earn and use Bells to buy the essentials, to get ahead you need to collect Nook Miles. You can collect these just by playing the game. Collecting bugs, catching fish, picking fruit, and crafting will all bag you valuable miles. Use them to pay off your Nook Inc. debt or buy extra goods and services. You can always check which activities will net you more Nook Miles. Just pull out your NookPhone and check the Nook Miles page.

IT'S LIKE: THE SIMS
■ There's nothing else quite like Animal Crossing, but The Sims is as close as it gets. Its Island Living expansion could even give Nook Inc. an idea or two.

TRY: RUNE FACTORY 4 SPECIAL
■ Mix the farming action of the Story of Seasons games with a fantasy RPG, and you get the much-loved Rune Factory series. This Switch remaster of the 3DS favorite is Rune Factory at its best.

LIVING THE DREAM

■ Don't get too obsessed with making progress on your island. Hang out with your new friends, go fishing, watch the stars, and just relax.

■ With time, Bells, and Nook Miles, your settlement can grow into a real town, with new stores arriving, town squares to relax in, and even its own museum to fill with interesting stuff.

■ You can also turn your tent into a house, and plant your own garden. You can even use the new construction tools to alter the landscape, and really make your island your own.

Rosie

Heeeeey! How ya doing?

■ Sometimes visitors may come to the island. Make friends and they might even join your neighborhood. Nook Inc. might also fly in new residents, so make sure you make everyone feel welcome.

■ If you share your Switch, the rest of your family can join the fun. There's only one island per Switch, but up to eight of you can share it, all living in your own tents or houses.

■ Before you know it, your island will be packed with new inhabitants, including some familiar Animal Crossing characters and some all-new friends. Find out what makes them tick, what they love, and what they hate, and you'll make the island an even better place to live!

TAKE A TRIP

■ Want a break away from your island? You can spend Nook Miles on Nook Mile Tickets for an exciting island tour. On these new islands, you'll find unique flowers, trees, fruit, bugs, and more—and you can bring them back home!

■ You can also use the airport to fly to another player's island, and see what they've been up to, what they've made, and how their island's growing. Or why not invite other players to come and explore your island? Up to eight players can roam around one island at a time.

Wilbur

Alright, we are two down and docked at the target island! Delta Oscar Delta Oscar is go.

BRAVELY DEFAULT II

ANOTHER MIGHTY RPG HITS THE SWITCH

If Bravely Default was the best RPG on the 3DS, then the Switch gives the series its chance to shine. It comes from the same studio that brought us Octopath Traveler, and uses a similar mix of gorgeous 3D backgrounds and retro characters to create its own cool style. And if it looks old-fashioned but with some modern twists, the same is true of the gameplay, which combines traditional turn-based battles with some smart defensive options.

It's the tale of a princess on the trail of four elemental stones, which, scattered around the world, are causing havoc across four distant lands. On her quest, she's joined by a mysterious sailor, a wandering scholar, and a hard-bitten mercenary, all with their own reasons to seek the stones. This has all the signs of an epic adventure—one of the biggest and best on the Switch!

QUICK TIPS:

DEFAULT

■ Make the most of the default and brave mechanics. When you default, you can soak up damage that would normally kill you, then dish out your own supercharged attacks.

CHOOSE YOUR WEAPONS

■ Each weapon will have different strengths and weaknesses when used by heroes with different jobs. When you're buying or swapping weapons, watch how the stats go up and down in the preview to the right.

TAKE TWO JOBS

■ Each character can have one primary job and one secondary job, giving you different skills and perks. Try different combinations of jobs on different characters to see what fits your play style.

PREPARE FOR BATTLE!

DEFAULT AND DEFEND
■ Bravely Default has turn-based combat like an old RPG, but there are some big differences. Pick default when it's time to send your hero into battle, and they'll go into a defensive pose and their DP will go up by one.

Shield Bash

MIGHTY MOVES
■ Each job brings its own special moves. For instance, while the Vanguard has a range of sword and shield combos, the Monk has awesome hand-to-hand attacks.

Strong Strike

BRAVELY ATTACK
■ You can then keep defaulting in the next round, attack as normal, or spend some of the DP you've banked on getting an extra attack or magic spell this round. You can store up several attacks, then unleash them in one furious move!

MAKE MAGIC
■ White and Black Mages bring spells to the party. While the White Mage's spells focus on healing and protection, the Black Mage is all about dealing damage.

SPECIAL ABILITIES
■ Each job also has a showstopping special ability, perfect for blasting tougher enemies to kingdom come!

FAST FACT:
Bravely Default II is confusingly the third game in the series, coming after Bravely Second: End Layer, which launched on the 3DS in 2016

Shakedown

IT'S LIKE: OCTOPATH TRAVELER
■ From the same studio as Bravely Default and its sequel, Octopath Traveler combines eight different fantasy adventures into one intertwining saga.

TRY: LOST SPHEAR
■ If you love retro Japanese RPGs, Lost Sphear is a modern epic that looks back to the glory days of Chrono Trigger and Final Fantasy VI.

BEST
MOBILE GAMES

Get your gaming to go with the best on iPhone, iPad, and Android

PLAY IT:
Android, iPad, iPhone

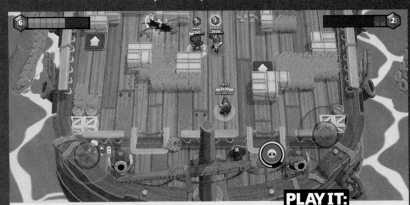

PLAY IT:
Android, iPad, iPhone

BRAWL STARS

■ When the makers of Clash of Clans and Clash Royale create a multiplayer shooter, you know they've got something special in mind. Part team deathmatch game, part battle royale, Brawl Stars looks like a simple, cuddly shooter. Keep playing, though, and you'll find tactics, skills, and a whole lot of mayhem inside its colorful bite-sized maps.

POKÉMON GO

■ It's the game that has gotten the world out of the house, trying to catch 'em all. Pokémon GO keeps getting better, with players teaming up for epic Raid Battles against rare Legendary Pokémon or taking on Team Rocket trainers when they occupy a Gym. Pokémon GO is the mobile gaming obsession that just won't go away.

PLAY IT:
Android, iPad, iPhone

NBA 2K20

■ Think you couldn't fit a sports game as big as NBA 2K20 onto a smartphone? Think again. It looks almost as good as it does on console, and the simplified controls help the gameplay flow. Best of all, it packs in almost all the modes, from the MyCareer story mode to the Run the Streets street ball game. Can anyone say slam dunk?

LEAGUE OF LEGENDS: WILD RIFT

■ One of the PC's biggest games has now gone mobile. Like the big-screen League of Legends, it's a multiplayer online battle arena, with a top lineup of champions and all the player vs. player action. The only difference is a smaller, tighter map, responsive touchscreen controls, and more thumb-friendly abilities and spell-casting.

PLAY IT:
Android, iPad, iPhone

SHADOWGUN WARGAMES

■ Look, it's basically Overwatch on mobile. It's a hero shooter with a range of different tank, damage, and support characters, each with their own special guns and powers, duking it out in teams on compact maps. It even looks like Overwatch. And that's fine, because if you love Overwatch—and who doesn't—you'll love this.

ASPHALT 9: LEGENDS

■ Even the world's worst drivers can still love Asphalt 9. There's a Touch Drive mode, where you don't even have to steer or brake! If you're a racing game fan, don't worry; this could be the most intense arcade racer on mobile, with incredible graphics, tracks set all around the world, and an amazing lineup of sports cars and supercars to drive.

PLAY IT:
Android, iPad, iPhone

PLAY IT:
Android, iPad, iPhone

SHADOWGUN
WAR GAMES

ALTO'S ODYSSEY

■ The adventurous snowboarder, Alto, has left snow behind for sand, but that's not going to stop him from speeding through the desert and sliding down the dunes at speed—or jumping rocks, grinding rope lines, and bouncing off balloons. Alto has the looks, the style, and the gameplay to keep you coming back for more.

PLAY IT:
Android, iPad, iPhone

▶

MARVEL STRIKE FORCE

■ This awesome squad-based RPG brings all your favorite Marvel stars together, to take on a rogue Kree warlord and his Hydra buddies. The trick to winning battles is to combine your powers in true Avengers style, and you can even mix your heroes and villains together for player vs. player matches against your friends.

PLAY IT:
Android, iPad, iPhone

MONUMENT VALLEY 2

■ Monument Valley was an instant smartphone puzzle classic. It had mind-warping optical illusion puzzles and some of the most stylish graphics around. Monument Valley 2 is even better, cranking up the puzzles, and adding more moving walkways and impossible paths, to create a game that makes your eyes happy while your brain hurts.

PLAY IT:
Android, iPad, iPhone

PLAY IT:
Android, iPad, iPhone

SKY: CHILDREN OF THE LIGHT

■ From the people who brought us Journey comes another classic adventure. Here, you run, glide, and slide through a series of strange landscapes, trying to find and heal trapped spirits. Sky is every bit as magical as Journey. But what makes it special is the way you can join forces with other players without ever saying a single word.

PLAY IT:
Android, iPad, iPhone

ODDMAR

■ Here's a brilliant old-school platformer in the style of the old Rayman games. As the world's only peace-loving Viking, you've got to leap, dash, hack, and slash your way through 24 amazing levels, where you'll battle monsters, get chased by trolls, and harness magical powers. Pinching odd ideas from platform gaming classics, Oddmar is a class act.

OCEANHORN

PLAY IT:
Android, iPad, iPhone

■ It's not hard to spot Oceanhorn's influences—it's basically a Zelda tribute game. Still, who cares when it looks this good and plays this well, especially when you'll never get the real deal on your phone. Explore, fight, and puzzle your way through ten hours of adventure, with the first part free to play.

BAD NORTH

PLAY IT:
Android, iPad, iPhone

■ Bad North looks like a simple, sweet strategy game, then turns into a battle for survival. It's up to you to defend your island from invading Vikings, moving your archers, swordsmen, and spearmen from one spot to another, ready to repel the next wave of marauders. At first, it's easy, but then the real warriors wade in. Prepare to cry.

PLAY IT:
Android, iPad, iPhone

FORTNITE: BATTLE ROYALE

■ The world's favorite battle royale doesn't lose much if you play on mobile, giving you all the build-and-blast action you'd find in the real deal. As long as your phone can handle the pace, it's a great way to play Fortnite on the move, with all the outfits, locations, weapons, and gadgets you'll find on console or PC—and it even works with a Bluetooth controller. It's still the king of the mobile battle royales.

PLAY IT:
iPad, iPhone

DONUT COUNTY

■ The game where you play a hole, roaming around Donut County, sucking up objects, people, and maybe even the whole dang place. The more that goes in, the bigger you get, and once you start combining objects and even spitting them out, the sky's the limit on the mayhem you can cause. Don't fight the weirdness—it's a hole lot of fun.

ORI AND THE WILL OF THE WISPS

THE LITTLE GUARDIAN SPIRIT IS A MIGHTY GAMING FORCE

Ori and the Blind Forest came out of nowhere to become one of the best-loved 2D platform adventures of this console generation. That's meant some high expectations for its sequel, but Ori and the Will of the Wisps is even better than we hoped! It takes everything good about Ori's first outing and builds it up into an epic adventure, with even more beautiful, hand-painted graphics and the kind of art you'd usually see in Japanese animated movies. If you're looking for a game that's like Hollow Knight meets Rayman meets *My Neighbor Totoro*, this is it.

Ori has grown as a hero for this second game, with new abilities, a different upgrade system, and a whole new approach to combat. And Ori will need them all to rescue Ku, the child of the giant owl, Kuro, from the first game. You'll have to face down deadly monsters, and survive a new and even more perilous forest. Luckily, Ori has the courage and the skills to survive.

QUICK TIPS:

PAY ATTENTION
■ Ori's world is full of hidden areas and secret routes that open up new spaces to explore. If you can't find a way in now, don't worry. You might come back later with a new ability.

FIGHT DIRTY
■ Even the most basic monsters can do a lot of damage, but you don't always have to fight them toe to toe. Lure them or bash them into a bank of thorns, and let the spikey stuff do its work.

CHAIN YOUR MOVES
■ The more progress you make, the more abilities you'll unlock. Look for ways to chain them together to reach new areas. If there's a gap you can't make by jumping, try a double-jump and a dash followed by a grapple.

SPIRIT SKILLS

SPIRIT EDGE
■ Ori starts the game defenseless, but that doesn't last for long. Your first ability, Spirit Edge, is a deadly blade with a vicious downward slash.

SPIRIT ARC
■ Your second weapon is a spirit bow firing arrows of light across the screen. Aim while you hold the button, then release. It doesn't do a lot of damage, but it will activate switches you can't reach.

SPIRIT SMASH
■ This mighty hammer is slower than the sword, but it does a lot more damage whenever it connects. Use it to squash bothersome bugs and bash other forest foes into next week.

FAST FACT:
Studio Ghibli's animated movies were a massive influence on the first Ori. One area was named in honor of *Nausicaä of the Valley of the Wind.*

DASH
■ Just when you're getting used to a double-jump move, Ori unlocks the Dash. It will help you leap across chasms full of spikey thorns, and dodge spirit-squashing block traps.

GRAPPLE
■ Unlock this ability, and Ori can lock onto lamps and other points of light, then slingshot through the air. The game pauses briefly while you aim and shoot, and it even works with projectiles coming in toward you.

USE THE SHARDS

■ Ori and the Blind Forest had a simple upgrade system, where you could develop Ori's abilities one by one. The sequel goes for a more flexible system based on shards. You'll find shards hidden away in different areas of the world—though they're often difficult to reach. Grab one, and it's added to your shard collection.

SPIRIT TRIALS

■ Some areas of the game have special portals that transport Ori away to a Spirit Trial. In these time trial challenges, you can race through the levels against recorded "ghosts" set down by your friends, giving you the chance to show off your awesome spirit moves.

■ There are dozens of shards to collect, but you can only have three of them active at any time. You can use them to customize Ori for the way you like to play, making the spirit more resistant to damage, ramping up attacks in combat, or even allowing Ori to stick to the walls.

■ Shards can also be upgraded, making them and their effects more powerful. You can buy upgrades—along with new shards—from the merchant Twillen, whom you can find in different spots around the world.

IT'S LIKE: ORI AND THE BLIND FOREST

■ Ori's first game hasn't lost its magic. It's not as big and the difficulty level gets harsh, but it's a brilliant, heartwarming platform adventure.

TRY: HOLLOW KNIGHT

■ These two games share a lot of the same influences and a similar style of gameplay, but Hollow Knight has its own strange atmosphere and an absorbing insect fantasy world.

BEAT THE BEASTS

■ Ori might be a small spirit in a big, bad world, but this hero is never short of courage. On your way to rescue your owl friend and discover your own strange history, you'll have to fight some fearsome monsters.

THE BEETLE
■ When this bad-tempered bug isn't charging at you, it's trying to pounce on you or breathing fire. Its thick armor can't cover the whole body, though. Dodge its fearsome charge, then hit it where it hurts.

THE WOLF
■ The wolf won't let you rest until it has you in its jaws, but Ori can turn the tables on the hairy brute. Revenge is best served flaming hot!

THE SPIDER
■ This eight-legged freak spits deadly venom and can't wait to get its fangs into our hero. You can damage it with arrows if you don't want to get too close to its eight beady eyes.

THE FIRE-BREATHING BUG
■ This creepy-crawly terror can release a stream of burning lava on command. Stay out of range and off the ground if you don't want to get your toes scorched.

TOP 10 ROBLOX GAMES

PRESS PLAY ON THESE CLASSICS—THEY'RE THE BEST OF THE BLOX!

1

DEN_S
THEME PARK TYCOON 2
■ Grab some friends and build your own theme park, then fill it with thrill rides and awesome roller coasters. When you're done, why not give them a try yourself? Loop the loop and twist around.

2

DUCKARMOR
Q-CLASH
■ Roblox does Overwatch in a mighty team-based shooter. With eight different clashers with their own unique weapons and abilities, it's a multiplayer blast and surprisingly close to the Overwatch real deal!

3

SCHWIFTY STUDIOS
MAD CITY
■ Join a crazy town full of cops, criminals, and superheroes. Rob the bank, drive a getaway car, or foil the robbers to earn cash for new vehicles and gadgets. Hit the streets and go nuts.

4

VCAFFY
DUNGEON QUEST
■ Gang up with your buddies to battle through dungeons and slay the evil bosses at the end. Whether you swing a magic sword or cast fireball spells, you'll grow more powerful as you level up.

5

DUED1
WORK AT A PIZZA PLACE
■ One of the first Roblox greats is still one of the best. Pack and deliver pizzas to the people of a hungry town. You can even take over the management in a tycoon game with extra cheese.

6

STICKMASTERLUKE
NATURAL DISASTER SURVIVAL
■ The floodwaters are rising, meteors are falling, the world is collapsing around your ears. How long can you survive each disaster—and will running around in circles really help?

7

STYLIS STUDIOS
PHANTOM FORCES
■ It's a Call of Duty–style shooter made in Roblox—and it's a whole lot better than that sounds. The maps and the moves come straight from the greats, and it's fast and fun to play.

8

PINK SLIME STUDIOS
LAWN MOWING SIMULATOR
■ Worn out from all that action? Try a little easy yardwork. Cut the grass, collect the flowers, and bag the cash, then splurge on cool new slime pets and mower upgrades.

9

CALLMEHBOB
ROYALE HIGH
■ Enroll in a fairy-tale high school, find a dorm, go to classes, and try out the different styles. You can head off to parties, trade items, and accessorize with the latest fairy wings.

10

THE VESTERIA TEAM
VESTERIA
■ It's not the only fantasy RPG on Roblox, but it's easily the most ambitious, with all the quests, monsters, loot, and dungeons of a mini-World of Warcraft. Grab your sword and join the adventure.

XBOX CLASSICS

The games that made Xbox—and you can play them all today on Xbox One

BURNOUT PARADISE

■ Nearly all of the Burnout games are great, especially if you like an arcade racer with a side order of destruction. Burnout Paradise took everything that was so great about them and made it work in an open world. You can explore every avenue and side street of Paradise City, winning races, wrecking rivals, and buying all the greatest rides—if only you can keep them in one piece. It's a playground for dangerous driving and heaven for racing fans.

2008

2006

VIVA PIÑATA

■ Between its Nintendo classics and the brilliant Sea of Thieves, Rare's biggest hit was this oddball creature sim where you tended a fantasy garden full of strange paper animals. You had to keep the piñatas fed and watered, give them somewhere nice to sleep, and help them make a family, while keeping out the mean "sour" piñatas and sorting out other threats. It's still a gentle, funny, and lovable game, with the most gorgeous, brightly colored stars.

PLAY IT:
You can find it and its sequel on Xbox Game Pass and the Microsoft Store

PLAY IT:
The original is backward compatible, but we think it's worth splurging for the brilliant 2018 Xbox One remaster

2003

PRINCE OF PERSIA: THE SANDS OF TIME

PLAY IT:
Release the prince from his Microsoft Store prison and play it on the Xbox One

■ Prince of Persia was a 1989 2D platform game with astounding, lifelike animation (for the time). In 2003, its creator, Jordan Mechner, went to work with Ubisoft on a game that would bring the prince up to date. Prince of Persia: The Sands of Time introduced the kind of parkour-style 3D platforming that we now see in everything from Tomb Raider to Assassin's Creed and Uncharted—and it did it in an amazing Arabian Nights adventure that has barely aged.

2008

FABLE II

■ The legendary Lionhead Studios created some of the Xbox's greatest games before it tragically bit the dust. None were better than Fable II, an awesome action RPG where your hero and their dog could wander the fantasy realms of Albion and fight against an ancient evil. It all took place in a reactive world, where you could play good, evil, or even stupid and become respected, feared, or mocked in return. The chance to have a family (or a really silly haircut) was just a bonus!

PLAY IT:
You can buy and download Fable II through Xbox Games Pass or the Microsoft Store

PLAY IT:
You can still find Blinx hiding out in the Microsoft Store

BLINX

■ Back in 2002, console mascots mattered. To go up against Mario, Crash Bandicoot, and Sonic, Microsoft bet on Blinx, a time-traveling cat who starred in the world's first 4D action game. Blinx didn't have the charm of his rivals, but the time-controlling gameplay was actually pretty cool, as you sped up, slowed down, recorded, and reversed time to make your way through some ingenious platform levels and solved tricky puzzles. It's not perfect, but it's crammed with ideas.

PORTAL 2

■ Between its dark sci-fi FPS games, Valve Software created this incredible first-person puzzler, where you're trying to escape the vast laboratories of a scientific research company while being harassed by a computer gone mad. Your only hope is an experimental weapon that creates portals you can pass through, and figuring out how to use those portals to dodge the lab's deadly perils could make your brain turn to mush. Lots of smart people think Portal 2 is one of the best games ever made.

2011

PLAY IT:
You can find Portal 2 in the Microsoft Store

PANZER DRAGOON ORTA

■ Sega's much-loved dragon-riding series first appeared on its Saturn console—and the hardware wasn't strong enough to handle a game this big. With the original Xbox, it found a console powerful enough to take the heat, resulting in a visual showcase for the Xbox that can still turn heads today. Hurtle through the stunning scenery, blast your enemies, and deal with the screen-filling bosses, then wonder why nobody makes anything like this now.

PLAY IT:
Not only is this available through the Microsoft Store and Games Pass, it's been enhanced for Xbox One!

LOST ODYSSEY

◼ Lost Odyssey is probably the best Japanese RPG that you've never played. Before the Xbox 360 launched, Microsoft spent huge amounts of money to get a new, incredibly ambitious game developed by some of the creative minds behind Final Fantasy. It took a long time, but the resulting game is a massive epic that pushed the console to its limits. Even today, it looks great and has a haunting tale to tell—and was one of the few games to rival the PS4-only Final Fantasy XII.

PLAY IT:
We haven't lost this odyssey. You can buy it from the Microsoft Store

2008

FORZA HORIZON

2002

◼ All the Forza games are classics, but especially the first Forza Horizon. It took the stunning graphics and lifelike handling from Forza Motorsport 3 and put them in a game that had more in common with an arcade racer like Need for Speed. Speeding around a shrunken Colorado is still a blast, whether you're driving the world's most gorgeous supercars or some turbo-powered, jacked-up muscle car. If you love Forza Horizon 4, you owe it to yourself to find out where it started.

PLAY IT:
It's another Xbox 360 game you can play through backward compatibility, though it's not on Xbox Games Pass or the Microsoft Store as we write

HALO 1–3

◼ You just knew the Master Chief would have to take the top spot! Halo didn't just launch the Xbox as a major gaming console—it also transformed what we thought a console FPS could be. The original is still a stone-cold classic, and with Halo 2 and Halo 3 the action only got bigger and better. Halo 3: ODST and Halo: Reach are nearly as essential, but it's impossible to imagine the Xbox without these three games.

2001 to 2007

PLAY THEM:
Get your hands on the beautifully remastered versions in the Halo: Master Chief Collection

PSYCHONAUTS

◼ Once upon a time, most 3D platform games were full of cute little characters, collecting cute things in cute little worlds. Then along came Psychonauts and everything went weird. The Xbox original took you deep into the minds of a crazy cast of oddballs and villains, where you might be exploring the fears of an overgrown fish or foiling a conspiracy involving spies and milkmen. Play it now, then get a load of this year's sequel.

PLAY IT:
Find the madness on the Microsoft Store

2005

2003

STAR WARS: KNIGHTS OF THE OLD REPUBLIC

■ Think Star Wars Jedi: Fallen Order is the best-ever Star Wars game? Get ahold of Knights of the Old Republic and think again. An epic RPG from BioWare—the makers of Mass Effect and Dragon Age—it's set thousands of years before the movies, but still captures just what makes them special. As a Jedi who has lost his memory, you can explore strange worlds, battle the Sith, and discover the truth behind old legends, all in a tale that will keep you hooked.

PLAY IT:
Download the best Star Wars prequel from the Microsoft Store

STREET FIGHTER IV **2008**

■ You can't ignore the game that put Capcom back on the fighting game throne. Street Fighter IV was its first successful effort to mix the comic-book styles and characters of the classic Street Fighter games with the 3D graphics Namco had mastered with the likes of Tekken and Soulcalibur. It was also the first Street Fighter in years that captured the turbocharged gameplay and sheer excitement of the original games. It's a beat-'em-up all-time great.

PLAY IT:
Download the enhanced Super Street Fighter IV: Arcade Edition from the Microsoft Store

2006

ROCKSTAR GAMES PRESENT TABLE TENNIS

■ Who would have thought it? A table tennis game from the makers of Grand Theft Auto? How on Earth could this be great? Yet Rockstar Table Tennis was one of the most fun and addictive sports games ever, with detailed graphics and fast-paced gameplay where you could almost feel the paddle in your hand. It also had a brilliant soundtrack, and a crowd that seemed to respond to every drive and backhand. Look, Rockstar, do we have to beg for a next-gen remake?

PLAY IT:
Download it straight from the Microsoft Store

GEOMETRY WARS: RETRO EVOLVED **2003**

■ This mighty retro shoot-'em-up began as a minigame, concealed inside Project Gotham Racing 2 on the original Xbox. But Geometry Wars was just too good to hide away, and when the Xbox 360 launched it was one of the first hits on Xbox Live Arcade. Its flashy, brightly colored graphics have stood the test of time and influenced a thousand other games. Yet it's the furiously addictive arcade gameplay that keeps you coming back for one more try.

PLAY IT:
You can still buy and play the original from the Microsoft Store, or buy Geometry Wars 3: Dimensions for your Xbox One

DESTROY ALL HUMANS!

PLAYING SPACE INVADERS WAS NEVER THIS MUCH FUN

Take a break from blasting aliens and find out what it's like on the other side! This remake of the 2005 cult classic puts you in the creepy silver suit of Crypto-137, a Furon secret agent let loose on 1950s Earth. Armed with a flying saucer, psychic powers, and an array of alien gadgets, you're on a mission to bring down the US government and harvest human brains.

It's great being the bad guy, collecting brains, abducting cows, and lifting cars with the power of your mind, but build up enough heat and you'll be in trouble, not just from the army but from Majestic, a sinister agency of men in black. Blast them, disintegrate them, and show them who's boss. Destroy them all!

QUICK TIPS:

LOW PROFILE
■ The more you're seen and the more trouble you cause, the more attention you'll get from the army and Majestic. Keep a low profile early on and focus on your missions.

COLLECT DNA
■ You need DNA to upgrade your abilities and unlock new areas. You can get it by completing missions, taking on optional challenges, and extracting puny human brains.

HUNT THE PROBES
■ Each area has dozens of probes hidden away. Track them down for easy DNA—and there are bonus rewards if you can find them all.

TOOLS OF
DESTRUCTION

FLYING SAUCER
■ Crypto's flying saucer isn't just for getting from A to B. You can use its Abduction beam to pick up pesky humans and their animals and vehicles, or kit it out with death rays and sonic cannons.

RAY GUNS AND ION BOMBS
■ Crypto's trusty Zap-O-Matic fires bolts of electricity, but before long he'll be packing Ion Bombs and the awesome Disintegrator.

ALIENS IN DISGUISE
■ Crypto's advanced psychic abilities can create "Holobob" disguises to impersonate humans, giving him access to secure locations. Just one problem—those Majestic clowns see right through them!

PSYCHOKINESIS
■ The Furon mind is more powerful than the weak human brain, allowing Crypto to lift and even throw large objects using nothing more than psychic power.

MIND CONTROL
■ Hypno-blast humans and you can distract them or send them to sleep. Both animals and humans can also be forced into dancing!

FAST FACT:
The original Destroy all Humans! spawned three sequels following Crypto's evil antics through 20 years of Earth's history.

IT'S LIKE: THE INCREDIBLE HULK: ULTIMATE DESTRUCTION
■ Like Destroy all Humans!, the best Hulk game ever was part of an explosion of open world games that arrived in the wake of GTA III, and has the same playful take on mass destruction.

TRY: JOURNEY TO THE SAVAGE PLANET
■ Looking for another game with a great world to explore and a fun retro sci-fi style? You can't beat this spectacular outer space adventure.

HALO INFINITE

IT'S NOT JUST THE COMBAT THAT'S EVOLVED

There have been nearly 20 years between the release of Halo: Combat Evolved and Halo Infinite, but time has been kind to the Master Chief. In fact, Earth's mightiest Spartan just keeps on looking better, as each Xbox brings new and more powerful hardware, and the studios develop more advanced graphics tech.

■ Halo: Combat Evolved and Halo 2 had some of the best graphics of any action game. Though the Chief's Spartan armor looks primitive by modern standards, its detailed joints and reflective visor were pretty advanced for the time.

■ With Halo Infinite, the Chief's armor has been modified to look slightly more like the original Combat Evolved suit. Both our hero and the armor have been through the wars—take a look at the burn damage on the breastplate and the worn-down edges and metal. This stuff isn't just for show!

■ The Master Chief got a much more realistic look for Halo 3 on the Xbox 360. There's much more detail in the armor, the weapons, and the Master Chief's helmet. Check out those battle-worn textures on the metal.

■ For Halo 5: Guardians on the Xbox One, the Chief got another shot of detail, with even more elements to the different armor pieces—it looks good in still shots, but check out all the animated parts when the game's in motion, if you get the chance.

FAST FACT:
The voice of the Master Chief, Steve Downes, has also voiced Star-Lord in an Avengers cartoon series and is a morning radio DJ in Chicago.

THE ENEMY
■ It's not just the Master Chief who's been enhanced over the years; the same thing has happened to everything and everyone in the Halo universe. Here are some Covenant Elites from Halo 2 in 2004, and here they are in Halo 5: Guardians, 11 years later!

WAY TO THE WOODS

CAN A DEER AND A FAWN RETURN LIFE TO A DEAD WORLD?

You don't always need a massive team to build an amazing game. Anthony Tan started Way to the Woods at just 16 years old and has spent the last four years working on it mostly on his own, with just some help on the animation and the music. A game that started out as a personal project became a trailer and then one of the most-hyped indie games for Xbox One.

Influenced by Journey and Studio Ghibli's animated movies, it's an adventure in which an adult deer and a fawn take a long journey through a world where the human race seems to have died out, leaving our cities empty and abandoned. On their way, they'll have to find food and shelter, solving simple puzzles, and using their natural abilities and magical powers to get past every obstacle standing in their way. Sounds weird? Maybe, but see it in action and it's a game full of wonder and real heart.

QUICK TIPS:

DON'T STARVE!
■ If you need food, charge and smash into a vending machine. You're guaranteed to get some goodies you can feed your deer and fawn.

DON'T RUSH IT
■ This isn't the kind of game you rush through. There's a lot to explore and a lot of puzzles to be solved. Take your time to try out different ideas—and don't spoil things by reaching for a walkthrough.

AMAZING ANTLERS
■ Those antlers aren't just for show. You can use them to break some surfaces or objects, while their strange powers can bring dead technology back to life.

THE LOST WORLD

THE WAY BACK HOME
■ One of the best things about Way to the Woods is how the animals are exploring a strange, abandoned world that we might just recognize. It's a very different take on the usual post-apocalyptic game!

FAST FACT:
Anthony is a massive fan of *Steven Universe* and persuaded Aivi & Surasshu, who wrote the show's music, to create new music for his game.

FRIENDS AND FOES
■ You're not as alone as you think. You'll meet cats, dogs, and a bunch of smaller critters. Some of your fellow beasts pose a threat, but you might be able to recruit others to help you. You're definitely going to meet some strange characters along your way.

RELICS OF THE PAST
■ This world is full of relics of humanity, from deserted railway stations and shopping malls to strange machines that you might be able to reactivate. Interacting with the world might help you understand what has happened to it.

SECRETS OF THE OOZE
■ You'll also keep coming across a thick, black goo. What is this dark and dangerous substance, and how can you get rid of it?

IT'S LIKE: ABZÛ
■ Journey is the obvious influence on Way to the Woods, but check out this amazing aquatic adventure, where you can dive deep to explore the ruins of an ancient civilization.

TRY:
LOST EMBER
■ Way to the Woods isn't the only brilliant indie game where you control an animal. Become a wolf who can possess other animals, and discover a magical world.

INDIE

ESSENTIALS

Looking for something different? Play these classic indie hits

CELESTE BY MATT MAKES GAMES INC.

■ Celeste looks back to the days when platform games were made of tiny levels, each one hard as nails. Even they, though, had nothing on this mountain-climbing saga. Playing Madeline, you have to get to the summit through over 600 screens, with the challenge level starting at Pretty Tricky, then escalating rapidly to Seriously, what?. Celeste's sweet pixel graphics and synth-heavy soundtrack help take away some of the pain.

STARDEW VALLEY BY ERIC BARONE

■ Don't you want a break from all that shooting, racing, looting, and monster slaying? How about a few weeks as a farmer in Stardew Valley, where you can raise crops and animals, head out for some fishing, or do a little mining, crafting, and cooking? You'll need to make crucial gear and supplies, while there's a whole village full of people to befriend, either by completing quests or picking the right gift. It's all so relaxing and so weirdly addictive, you might never want to leave.

SABLE BY SHEDWORKS

■ Here's another indie hit with an arty style, this time based on the clean lines and muted colors of classic European comic-books. It's a young girl's journey of discovery across the surface of an alien desert planet, where you'll have to explore ancient cities and abandoned starships, while digging deep into the world's strange history. With plenty of action, drama, and discovery, it's a giant-sized adventure from a tiny team.

DEAD CELLS BY MOTION TWIN

■ How's this for an unlikely hero: You're a weird slime creature from an alchemist's laboratory, seizing control of dead bodies in a dungeon and using them to fight your way through an island full of monsters. You'll keep dying, but earn cells and you can buy upgrades to boost your skills next time. Dead Cells is a retro adventure with a modern Dark Souls twist, and as ghoulishly exciting as they come.

PLAY IT:
PC, Mac, PS4, Xbox One, Nintendo Switch

PLAY IT:
PC, PS4, Xbox One, Nintendo Switch

SLAY THE SPIRE BY MEGA CRIT

■ First, we had collectible card games like Magic: The Gathering. Then we had video game versions, like Hearthstone. What Slay the Spire does so brilliantly is take them and mash them up with a simple RPG that changes each time you die— which you will. A lot. Keep building your deck with each try, and you'll get more cards to play in battle. Keep playing and slaying until you reach the top.

PLAY IT:
PC, PS4, Xbox One, Nintendo Switch, iOS, Android

RIME BY TEQUILA WORKS

■ Hours in the playing, but years in the making, Rime feels like a cross between Sony's classic Ico and Nintendo's The Legend of Zelda games. As a young boy stranded on a mysterious island, you'll have to solve puzzles, navigate crumbling ruins, and escape wild creatures as the weather turns stormy. Come for the gorgeous cartoon graphics, stay for a game with brains and heart.

PLAY IT:
PC, Mac, PS4, Xbox One, Nintendo Switch

UNTITLED GOOSE GAME BY HOUSE HOUSE

■ There's a goose on the loose—and it's up to no good! As the bad bird of the title, it's up to you to honk and flap your way through an English village while being about as mean as possible to the locals. Grab their food, break their stuff, drive them to hide inside a phone booth—you've got a checklist full of bad deeds to be done. Mean-natured but weirdly lovable, it's no surprise it's an instant classic.

CRYPT OF THE NECRODANCER BY BRACE YOURSELF GAMES

■ Here's an action RPG with a difference, because while you're exploring clever, random dungeons, swords and sorcery won't save your life. Instead, you'll have to rely on your sense of rhythm, dancing your way through the skeletons and zombies to the beat of an irresistible soundtrack. A game so good that Nintendo called its makers in to create a Zelda version, the just-as-brilliant Cadence of Hyrule.

PLAY IT:
PC, PS4, Xbox One, Nintendo Switch, iOS

PLAY IT:
PC, Xbox One, Nintendo Switch

CUPHEAD BY STUDIOMDHR

■ Your average retro action game might look back to the 1980s, but Cuphead has the 1930s in its sights. The first thing that grabs you is the visuals, inspired by classic 1930s cartoons and using traditional hand-drawn art and animation. But it's the brutally difficult gameplay that will keep you coming back, as you battle through each level and some incredibly challenging bosses. See it to believe it, then pray you make it through.

OVERCOOKED BY GHOST TOWN GAMES

■ Play an overworked chef in some crazy kitchens in this magnificent, manic co-op hit. Up to four of you work together to prepare meals in bizarre circumstances, pushing to complete a minimum number of orders while dodging dangers like moving counters or a busy road. It's chaos even when you work together, and plain carnage when you don't, as pans catch fire and orders pile up. Can't take the heat? Run out of the kitchen.

PLAY IT:
PC, PS4, Xbox One, Nintendo Switch

THE STEAMWORLD SERIES BY IMAGE & FORM

■ The SteamWorld games are so good—and so different—that you can't pick out just one of them. SteamWorld Dig really started things off, combining weird western sci-fi with a classic 2D platform adventure, but since then we've had the shootout strategy of SteamWorld Heist and the card-battle RPG, SteamWorld Quest. Who knows what's next from SteamWorld? Whatever it is, it's going to be great.

PLAY IT:
PC, PS4, Xbox One, Nintendo Switch

HOLLOW KNIGHT
BY TEAM CHERRY

■ An epic adventure at an ant-sized scale, Hollow Knight takes you through an ancient, ruined kingdom of insect heroes and villains. Here, you'll explore strange underground realms, slashing through crazed insect enemies as you evolve new powers and skills. Hollow Knight is an indie update of classic 2D platform adventures like Castlevania and Super Metroid, but it brings them up to date.

PLAY IT:
PC, PS4, Xbox One, Nintendo Switch

JOURNEY BY THATGAMECOMPANY

■ Where do we start? With Journey's atmospheric abstract graphics, which have influenced a hundred indie games? Or how about the journey itself, where you start in the desert, exploring ancient ruins, then make your way through to sunken cities and dark caverns to the mountain you glimpsed at the beginning? Maybe it has to be the multiplayer, where you team up with other players without ever exchanging any words? Either way, it's magical.

PLAY IT:
PC, PS4, Xbox One

PLAY IT:
PC, PS4, iOS

OUTER WILDS BY MOBIUS DIGITAL

■ You're an astronaut camping in the wilder parts of space, but the solar system you're exploring is 22 minutes from disaster. But before the sun collapses, you can try to find out what's going on—and you'll keep waking up 22 minutes before the explosion until you do. Outer Wilds is one ingenious sci-fi mystery adventure with a clever time loop, and it will keep you coming back again and again and again and again…

ROCKET LEAGUE BY PSYONIX

■ Rocket League came from nowhere to become one of the biggest gaming hits of the last few years. It's basically soccer played with a giant-sized ball in rocket-powered cars, but that doesn't really do justice to the handling, the tactics, the moves, or the spectacle and speed—which have all made Rocket League a major eSport. The game keeps growing and the action just gets better, so hit the field and see what the fuss is all about.

PLAY IT:
PC, PS4, Xbox One, Nintendo Switch

WARCRAFT III: REFORGED

THE FANTASY BATTLE GAME TO END THEM ALL

Along with Command and Conquer, Warcraft created a new style of strategy war game. Instead of politely taking turns to command your troops, you controlled them with clicks of the mouse in real time. Mix that in with great graphics and pounding, movie-style soundtracks, and you had a game that was a blast to play.

Warcraft set the stage for StarCraft, World of Warcraft, and all their imitators, not to mention two cracking sequels. And now the best of those—Warcraft III—is back with a new coat of paint. The graphics have been rebuilt for today's PCs, and the heroes and villains have never looked better. If you've never played through the superb single-player campaign, now's your chance. It's a classic that will fill you in on the rich history of Azeroth, and you also get the Frozen Throne expansion and the all-time great multiplayer mode. Rally your army and prepare for war!

QUICK TIPS:

PLAY THE PROLOGUE
■ The orc prologue campaign does a great job of explaining how you build a base, recruit and upgrade units, and command them in battle. Play through the whole thing before you do anything else.

USE YOUR HEROES
■ The hero characters in Warcraft III have special abilities and level up as they earn experience in battle. Use them to attack tough enemy units or heal and support your other troops.

MASTER THE KEYBOARD
■ You can play Warcraft III almost completely using the mouse, but you'll do things faster if you can learn a few keyboard shortcuts. This goes double as your army grows.

BUILD AND BATTLE!

BUILD YOUR BASE
■ You need a base to build an army. Different units—your different types of warrior or wizard—need different buildings to produce them. Other buildings will upgrade your troops or unlock more powerful types.

HARVEST GOLD AND LUMBER
■ Your buildings and your army need lumber and gold, so collect plenty of both! Each army has its own worker units. Select them and click on a resource, and they'll keep harvesting it until it's gone.

TRAIN YOUR TROOPS
■ As soon as you've built a barracks for your troops, you need to start recruiting your army. You'll need to go out and defeat hostile forces—and defend your growing base from their attacks!

FAST FACT:
Defense of the Ancients, the game that went on to inspire League of Legends and Dota 2, began life as an unofficial custom game in Warcraft III!

BRING IN THE HEROES
■ Your hero characters make good leaders for your army, which you can divide into smaller groups. Each hero has special abilities to attack the enemy or support your units. This sorcerer can summon fierce water elementals and call in a vicious blizzard attack.

DESTROY THE ENEMY
■ Once you've built a good-sized army, you can get out there and complete your mission. You might have to fight a certain enemy or escape a dangerous situation, or you might have to destroy the enemy's base.

IT'S LIKE: STARCRAFT II
■ StarCraft II took the Warcraft gameplay into a dark sci-fi universe, where space marines battled with two awesome alien races and their own homegrown evil empire.

TRY: HALO WARS 2
■ No Halo fan should be without this strategy game, which takes the best bits of Warcraft and StarCraft and pulls them into the Halo universe. Can you hold off the Covenant?

THE GAMES THAT MADE
GAMING

Take a trip back through gaming's past with the games that got us where we are today

```
SCORE<1>  HI-SCORE  SCORE<2>
  0410      0000
```

```
3                        CREDIT 00
```

SPACE INVADERS
TAITO

■ Space Invaders wasn't the first video game, but it's the one that kicked off the whole phenomenon. In the space of four years, it made nearly four billion dollars and led to a flood of electronic games appearing in arcades, bars, and fairgrounds around the world, then went on to quadruple sales of the Atari 2600—the first major games console. While Pong and Spacewar! came before it, the video game as we know it started here.

1980

PAC-MAN
NAMCO

■ By 1980, the arcades were filling up with early classics, but while most were all about shooting, Pac-Man gave us something different. Here was a crazy maze chase game where our hero guzzled dots while being chased by ghosts. Plus, for a yellow blob with nothing but a mouth and eyes, Pac-Man had a lot of charm. Sequels featuring the Pac-Man family followed, along with loads of merchandise. Gaming's first real hero was born.

HISTORY

WIZARDRY
SIR-TECH

1981

■ In the early 1980s, the first home computers were running text-based adventures and simple arcade hits, but then some clever coders figured out ways to use their computers to run the kind of Dungeons & Dragons adventures

they were playing at home. Ultima was hugely influential, inspiring a wave of American role-playing games, but Wizardry made waves both in the US and Japan, inspiring everything from The Elder Scrolls to Dragon Quest and Final Fantasy.

GAUNTLET
ATARI

1985

■ Gauntlet had a different take on Dungeons & Dragons. Instead of turning it into a complex computer RPG, it transformed it into a fast-paced fantasy arcade game. The big shift here was that four players could fight through the game together,

playing a barbarian warrior, wizard, Valkyrie, and elf, using the four joysticks built into the cabinet. As a bonus, it was one of the first games to use speech. As the arcades filled with "Warrior is about to die," we were busy playing the first great co-op game.

ELITE
ACORNSOFT

1984

■ In Britain, the BBC Micro was a home computer aimed at budding programmers and used in schools. It wasn't much of a games machine. This didn't stop two young programmers—David Braben and Ian Bell—from creating Elite for it. In Elite, you played a pilot, flying from star system to star system, fighting space pirates and trading rare goods, using a new style of 3D graphics. In giving you the freedom to explore and work inside or against the law, it became the original open world adventure.

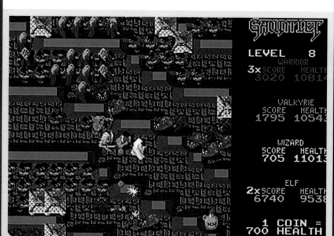

1986

OUTRUN
SEGA

■ Before OutRun, racing games were pretty basic. You drove a car along a featureless track, dodging other cars with the gas pedal floored. OutRun was a racing game with style. For a start, you drove a red Ferrari with the top down and the hero's girlfriend's hair waving in the breeze. You also drove it along cool coastal roads, over hills, and through the mountains, weaving through the traffic as you went. OutRun made driving an adventure.

1986

METROID
NINTENDO

■ When it was released in 1986, Metroid didn't look all that special. There were other platform games featuring cool space warriors blasting at aliens on every video game system going. Yet Metroid was different. It wasn't just about shooting, but exploration and discovery, where you couldn't access parts of the space pirates' base until you'd found or won the right equipment. Games from the Castlevania series right through to Hollow Knight and Star Wars Jedi: Fallen Order owe it a huge debt.

1987

MANIAC MANSION
LUCASARTS

■ In 1985, two game developers for George Lucas's games company, Lucasfilm Games, started work on a new style of adventure game. Where previous games had asked you to input text to tell your hero what to do, Maniac Mansion had you clicking icons. It was cinematic and crammed with silly dialogue—and it was funny! Maniac Mansion started a string of classic adventures, like The Secret of Monkey Island and Grim Fandango, that changed the way we talked in games.

JOHN MADDEN
FOOTBALL
ELECTRONIC
ARTS

■ Named after the legendary coach and commentator, John Madden Football revolutionized the sports game. Before it, even the best sports games tended to be simple arcade-style action games, but Madden brought in the challenges and tactics of real-world football, making a game fans couldn't put down. The series is still scoring touchdowns

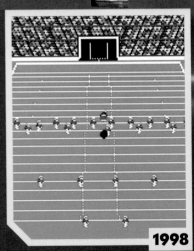

1998

over 20 years later, and has influenced every sports game going.

SIMCITY
MAXIS

1989

■ Before SimCity, most big strategy games were about war or conquering the stars. SimCity brought things right back down to Earth by putting you in charge of a growing city and asking you to meet its needs. You had to sort out the water suppliers, keep the traffic moving, and build areas for people to live, shop, and work. And if that wasn't tough enough, your city could be hit by fire, tornadoes, or even a giant monster lizard! The game that started theme park sims, transport sims, and more—not to mention The Sims itself!

STREET FIGHTER II
CAPCOM

■ By 1990, a handful of teams had tried their best to make the one-on-one fighting game work, but while Capcom struggled with the first Street Fighter, it succeeded with the sequel. Street Fighter II introduced everything that's great about the modern fighting game, from the overblown characters and silly storylines to the

special moves and clash of strikes, blocks, and counters. Even when Tekken and Virtua Fighter dragged the beat-'em-up into the 3D age, they couldn't escape the influence of Capcom's classic.

1991

SONIC THE
HEDGEHOG
SEGA

1991

■ You could argue that Sonic the Hedgehog isn't that influential. After all, it started out as Sega's response to Mario. But Sonic took the platform game and added speed, spectacle, and crazy thrills, along with a hedgehog hero with a cool, rebellious streak. Even more than Mario, Sonic showed that video game heroes could be stars, and that games could be blockbuster hits, causing fans to line up around the block to buy them.

THE LEGEND OF ZELDA SERIES
NINTENDO

■ If you're looking for a series that keeps changing gaming history, it's hard to beat The Legend of Zelda. The first game was a fun fantasy adventure with some great exploration, but not as revolutionary as the original Super Mario Bros. The second was a side-scrolling misfire. With its 1991 Super Nintendo debut, though, A Link to the Past, the series had hit its stride. You could get

out and explore the world of Hyrule in an ingenious adventure, where you could switch between two dimensions. It helped create a whole new style of fantasy adventure with an open world feel.

1998's Ocarina of Time did it again, not just making The Legend of Zelda work as a 3D game, but introducing a whole range of quests and activities that made Hyrule feel

like a living, breathing world. 2002's The Wind Waker gave us more with a cinematic feel and a brilliant Disney cartoon style. And while 2017's Breath of the Wild hasn't been so influential, it's showed how Nintendo can take ideas from other open world games then make something that feels even more open and free to explore and write your own story than any game before.

1986-2020

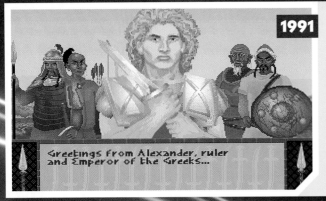

Greetings from Alexander, ruler and Emperor of the Greeks...

1991
SID MEIER'S CIVILIZATION
MICROPROSE

■ From the day it was released, Sid Meier's Civilization made it clear that it was a more ambitious style of strategy game. You could start your own civilization and transform it into an empire, taking it all the way from the stone age to the space race and off toward the stars. The historical angle made it twice as interesting—and also slightly educational—even if you had Gandhi squaring off against Napoleon and Genghis Khan! Epic strategy started here.

SUPER MARIO KART
NINTENDO

■ Super Mario Kart is a great example of how Nintendo uses the power of a new console, by using the cool Mode 7 feature of the Super NES, to make a new kind of 3D racing game. And Super Mario Kart wasn't your normal racer, either. Here, grabbing weapons and using them to bash your rivals was more important than speed. Mario Kart was and is a brilliant, brutally competitive party game featuring some of Nintendo's biggest stars, setting the scene not just for future kart racers, but Mario Party, Super Smash Bros., and more.

DAYTONA USA
SEGA

■ Having revolutionized the arcade racing game with high-speed 3D graphics in Virtua Racing, Sega went one step further with its follow-up, Daytona USA. The revolutionary graphics created cars that looked like real cars racing on an amazing recreation of the Daytona International Speedway, and the awesome speeds and fluid handling made it as good to play

1993

as it was to watch. With Namco's rival game, Ridge Racer, Daytona USA set the pace for racing games to come.

1993

DOOM
ID SOFTWARE

■ Doom wasn't the first FPS—the team at iD made Wolfenstein 3D before that—but it's definitely the most influential. It was scary, violent, and not at all suitable for kids, but its incredible 3D graphics and gruesome heavy metal sci-fi art helped make it one of the most exciting games anyone had ever played. Doom laid down the template for every FPS from Halo through to Call of Duty and Destiny—and it's still going strong today.

1994

NEED FOR SPEED
ELECTRONIC ARTS

■ By the early 1990s, you had two types of racing game. On the one hand, you had arcade racers with simple handling. On the other hand, more complex simulation games based on NASCAR, IndyCar, or Formula One. Need for Speed took the arcade racer and let you drive real cars with more realistic handling—and with the amazing graphics made possible by new 3D gaming consoles. It created one of the great racing series and cleared the road for Gran Turismo and Forza Motorsport.

WIPEOUT
PSYGNOSIS

■ With Ridge Racer and Tekken, the PlayStation had its first big games, but Sony wanted something to show that this wasn't just another console, but the start of something huge. With its flashy graphics, intense speeds, and pounding electronic dance music, Wipeout did just that. Suddenly, games weren't something that only kids played, but something everyone from your dad to the world's coolest DJs could enjoy.

1995

1996

TOMB RAIDER
CORE DESIGN

■ Tomb Raider proved that Nintendo wasn't the only one who could pull off a 3D platform game, and also introduced a new kind of gaming hero—someone who wasn't a cute critter or a sword-wielding elf, but a pistol-packing woman with cool style and acrobatic moves. Lara Croft became a virtual celebrity, and the games have inspired many other blockbusters, including Uncharted, Prince of Persia: The Sands of Time, and even Star Wars Jedi: Fallen Order.

MINECRAFT
MOJANG

■ In 2009, a Swedish developer called Markus Persson released an unfinished test version of an experimental game where players had to survive in a blocky sandbox world. They mined blocks of wood and rock to craft workbenches, furnaces, and shelters, which they could then use to craft weapons and equipment to help them survive the dangerous nights.

What really took off, though, wasn't just the survival angle, but the way you could use blocks to build anything you liked. Players went crazy for all this creative stuff. They built their own dream houses or secret hideouts. They rebuilt famous buildings from the world's biggest cities or their favorite books and movies. They even created their own weird worlds. What's more, the game has never stopped developing and changing, even 10 years after its release. The result? Minecraft is now the single bestselling video game of all time. 180 million players can't be wrong!

2009–2020

POKÉMON RED AND BLUE
NINTENDO

■ Pokémon changed gaming twice. First, by creating a whole new style of RPG that was more about exploring and collecting than just combat, where you could build up a team of little monsters, train them, and trade and battle them. Second, by becoming a massive TV and film phenomenon, spawning series, movies, spin-off games, and more. No other game has done this as successfully before or since—and from Pokémon GO to Pokémon Detective Pikachu, it's still going strong.

1996

FINAL FANTASY VII
SQUARESOFT

1997

■ Japanese RPGs were huge before 1997—but only in Japan. With Final Fantasy VII, Square made the rest of the world wake up. With its epic storyline, dramatic cinematic scenes, and lovable characters, it grabbed hold of players and kept them obsessed for weeks, opening the way for future Final Fantasy games, but also Dragon Quest, Fire Emblem, the Tales series, and more.

EVERQUEST
SONY ONLINE
ENTERTAINMENT

■ Big RPG games were one thing, but EverQuest made them multiplayer and took them online. The first big massive multiplayer online RPG, it set players loose in the fantasy world of Norrath, and had them questing, slaying monsters, and finding and crafting cool new gear. To succeed, though, you had to work with other players, joining them in massive monster battle raids and big group adventures. EverQuest built the foundations for today's big online hits, from World of Warcraft to Destiny.

METAL GEAR
SOLID
KONAMI

■ You knew you were onto something special from the first few minutes of Metal Gear Solid, with a sequence that could have come straight from a James Bond movie. Konami introduced the world to one of gaming's greatest heroes, Solid Snake, and a cinematic style of spy game, where sneaking worked better than shooting and something strange was always around the corner. With its weird, over-the-top villains and unpredictable storylines, Metal Gear Solid transformed the action game.

1998

1999

HALO: COMBAT EVOLVED
BUNGIE/MICROSOFT

■ In 2001, many people still thought that only the PC could do a really classic shooter. Halo blew that out of the water, nailing the controls and sorting out how you drove vehicles or switched between weapons, then delivering a heart-pounding sci-fi action game. Halo II did it again three years later by adding online multiplayer. Microsoft wanted to define the Xbox as the most advanced console ever. Halo did it in style.

2001

2006

WII SPORTS
NINTENDO

■ When Nintendo designed a revolutionary new, motion-controlled console, it had the perfect game to show it off. Wii Sports gave us tennis you could play by swinging a virtual racket, and baseball where you swung a virtual bat. You could bowl just like you would in real life, and even box by punching with the Wiimote and Nunchuk controllers clenched in your fists. This was the kind of game that everyone could play, and while motion controls aren't as big as they used to be, we wouldn't like to bet against a comeback.

2009

ANGRY BIRDS
ROVIO

■ There were mobile phone games before Angry Birds, but it took those catapulting birds and egg-napping pigs to bring smartphone gaming to the masses. Its controls were perfect for touchscreens, and figuring out how to use your bird lineup to get rid of the egg-napping porkers delivered puzzles that players loved. At one point, it seemed that everyone from schoolkids to politicians and TV stars were hooked. Even grandmas and grandpas couldn't resist just one more try!

THE SUPER MARIO SERIES
NINTENDO

■ No series has changed gaming history like the Super Mario series—and no one person has changed it more than Shigeru Miyamoto. Miyamoto took the basic platform game ideas he'd developed for Donkey Kong and Mario Bros. in the arcade to produce a defining game for the Nintendo Entertainment System (NES): the first side-scrolling action game with different levels, boss battles, power-ups, and all the stuff we've come to expect.

Since then, the Mario games have kept on mixing things up. Super Mario Bros. 3 was bigger and more sophisticated. Super Mario World on the Super NES let you ride on dinosaurs and gave you more choice over where you traveled next. Then Super Mario 64 showed gamemakers exactly how to make a 3D platform game, with controls that felt natural and a whole 3D world to explore. Super Mario Galaxy added motion controls to the mix, while New Super Mario Bros. U and Super Mario 3D World made Mario as great for four players as it was for one. From Super Mario Odyssey to Super Mario Maker 2, this is a series that can't stop inventing new ways to have fun.

1985-2020

DAUNTLESS

SLAY THE MONSTERS, SAVE THE CITY

The world of Dauntless has it bad. Some kind of magical disaster has shattered the world into floating chunks of land, held up by a mystic energy, Aether, that's the only thing between its people and extinction. But an even worse peril has emerged. Massive, powerful monsters—the Behemoths—have crawled onto the surface, hungry for the Aether and threatening all survivors.

As a slayer, it's up to you to join the fight against these gargantuan critters, hunting them down and stopping them for good them with your swords, axes, hammers, pistols, spears, and magic gauntlets. Fell the beasts and you can use their hides and bones for stronger armor and tougher weapons, to take on your next hunt. We know, it sounds a lot like Monster Hunter, but it's faster-paced, easier to get into, and—best of all—free to play, with the focus on fun co-op action. You've got to work together to bring those Behemoths down!

STUDY THE BEHEMOTHS
■ Each Behemoth has its own attack patterns and its own weak spots. Learn what these are—and figure out when you need to dodge—and you'll take less damage and do more to the monster.

LIGHT THE LANTERN
■ Early in the game, you can start crafting lanterns. When activated, these give powerful perks to you and nearby teammates. Remember to use and upgrade them. You'll need them for the tougher fights.

HOLD ONTO YOUR REVIVES
■ For every hunt, you'll have three revive tonics, but don't use them too quickly. Revive your teammates and trust them to help you. Save the revives for situations where you're all in danger.

BATTLE THE BEHEMOTHS

SHRIKES
■ This feathered bad boy is part eagle, part bear, part owl and all trouble. Watch out for its slicing talons, but try to hit it in the middle of its glide attacks.

EMBERMANES
■ Cross a wolf with a rhino and a fire-breathing dragon, and you've got Dauntless's hottest target. Embermanes have brutal charge moves and a nasty fireball attack, so stay mobile and keep dodging.

QUILLSHOTS
■ Armadillo meets giant porcupine in this vicious Behemoth. Watch out for its super-sized quills, which it can fire at range—or, better still, smash them before they can be used on you.

FAST FACT:
Dauntless supports cross-play across the Xbox One, PS4, PC and Switch versions, so you can play with your friends whatever their console.

SKARN
■ These thin-skinned lizards can encase themselves in rocky armor, which they'll then use to roll over you and crush you. Break the shell, then hack away at the beast underneath. And don't forget to dodge!

DRASK
■ The Drask is a huge electric alligator monster with a range of nasty shock attacks. Dodge the lightning, try to stay away from its teeth, and hit it from the side. It really doesn't like fire attacks.

IT'S LIKE: MONSTER HUNTER: WORLD
■ Even the Dauntless team have admitted to being Monster Hunter fans, though Dauntless's Behemoths and faster combat give the game a style of its own.

TRY: DESTINY 2
■ If you're looking for an action-packed co-op experience, it's hard to beat Destiny 2. Bungie's classic has its own big monsters to slay, and the core game is now free to play.

2021 GAME ON!

GLOSSARY

4K
■ A screen or image with an ultra-high definition resolution, giving the picture even more detail than high definition (HD).

Achievement
■ An award added to your online profile for completing goals or objectives in a game.

A.I.
■ Artificial Intelligence. Intelligent behavior simulated by a computer to, for instance, control how enemies behave toward a player or control other players on your team in a sports game.

AR
■ Augmented reality. A game or smartphone app that mixes real-world images from the camera with digital text and graphics.

Avatar
■ The character that represents the player in a game.

Battle royale
■ A type of action game where 60 or more players are dropped onto a single, large map and fight until just one survives.

Beat-'em-up
■ A fighting game, where two or more fighters battle in hand-to-hand combat.

Beta
■ An early version of the game often released to some players before a game launches, to check that the game works as it should.

Boss
■ A bigger, tougher enemy that players have to fight at the end of a level or mission in a game.

Campaign
■ A series of levels or objectives connected by some kind of story, usually making up the single-player mode of a game.

Camping
■ Hanging around in a single spot in a multiplayer action game in the hope of racking up easy kills.

CCG
■ Collectible card game. A style of game based on real-world card games, where players collect an army of cards and use them to battle other players.

Checkpoint
■ A point in a game where your progress is saved. If you die, you'll return to the checkpoint.

Cloud
■ An online service you can access from different consoles and computers in different places, allowing you to store or share saved games or even stream whole games.

Combo
■ In a fighting game or action game, a series of button presses that triggers a hard-hitting attack or counterattack.

Controller
■ The device used to control games when connected to a games console, through a mix of analogue sticks, digital D-pads, triggers, and buttons.

Co-op
■ A game or game mode where players can work together to complete objectives or win the game.

Cosplay
■ A fun hobby where people create amazing hand-crafted costumes to dress up as characters from their favorite games.

CPU
- Central processing unit. The main processor of a computer or games console that does most of the work of running games.

Crafting
- Using materials collected within a game to make useful items, armor, or weapons.

Cutscene
- An animated sequence or video sequence in a game, used to build atmosphere or tell the story.

Deathmatch
- A game mode where players fight against each other, competing for the highest number of kills.

DLC
- Downloadable content. Additional items, characters, or levels for a game that you can buy and download as extras.

DPS
- Damage per second. The amount of damage a character or weapon can dish out within a second. Can also refer to a character or class of hero who does a lot of damage quickly.

Easter egg
- A secret feature or item that's been hidden in a game, either for fun or as a reward for observant fans.

Endgame
- A part of a game that you can carry on playing after you've completed the main campaign or story.

eSports
- Electronic sports. The use of games or game modes for competition between highly skilled players, much like a regular sport. eSports have their own teams, leagues, and tournaments with big cash prizes.

F2P
- Free to play. A game that's free to download and play, though fans may pay for extra items, heroes, and missions.

FPS
- First-person shooter. A style of game where players move around a map, shooting enemies from a first-person perspective, with a view straight from the hero's eyes.

Frame rate
- The speed at which still frames replace each other to create a moving image on the screen. The higher the frame rate, the smoother the game looks and plays.

GPU
- Graphics processing unit. The chip inside a computer or console that turns instructions from the game software into 2D or 3D graphics you can see on the screen.

Griefing
- An activity in a multiplayer game where one player attacks other players repeatedly, to annoy them or discourage them from playing.

Grinding
- Doing slightly dull and repetitive activities in a game to make your character more powerful and the game slightly easier.

HDR
- High dynamic range. A technique used to give you deeper blacks, brighter whites, and a wider range of richer colors on your screen.

Indie game
- Short for independent. A game created by a small team of developers—or even a single developer.

eSports

CPU

JRPG

■ Japanese role-playing game. A game with the kind of gameplay and graphics you'd expect from a Final Fantasy, Persona, or Dragon Quest game.

Lag

■ A delay in response during online gaming, so that there's a short pause between the player taking an action and that action being shown on screen.

Leaderboard

■ An in-game chart that shows the highest scores or shortest times in a challenge or activity.

Level

■ A portion or chapter of the game set in one area and with a beginning, an end, and a series of goals and challenges in-between.

Map

■ An in-game map to help you find objectives, or a level where players can fight in a multiplayer game.

Metroidvania

■ A style of game influenced by the old Metroid and Castlevania series, where players roam round a huge game world and find gadgets or costumes that enable them to explore new areas that were previously locked.

MMO

■ Massive multiplayer online. A type of game where you share an online game world with dozens or even hundreds of other players, all playing at the same time.

MOBA

■ Multiplayer online battle arena. A multiplayer game where two teams of players select champions and go into battle for a series of objectives until one team wins.

Mod

■ Short for modification. A small bit of software or new art, or a new map that modifies an existing game, adding features or improving the way it looks.

Noob

■ A new and inexperienced player without the skills and knowledge of an experienced gamer.

NPC

■ Non-player character. A character in a game controlled by the computer. NPCs often provide guidance, sell goods, or help tell the story of the game.

Open world

■ A style of game where players are free to explore one or more large areas and try out different activities, rather than complete one level after another.

Patch

■ An update to a game that fixes bugs or adds new features.

Platformer

■ Platform game. A type of game where you run across a series of platforms or a challenging landscape, leaping over gaps and obstacles, and avoiding or defeating enemies in your path.

Port

■ A version of a game made for one console or computer that's been converted to run on another.

PvE

■ Player vs. environment. An online game or game mode where players work together to beat computer-controlled enemies.

MMO

WORLD OF WARCRAFT

BATTLE FOR AZEROTH

Metroidvania

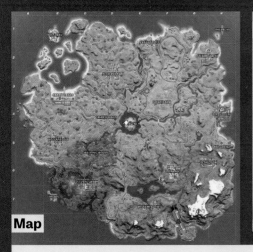

Map

VR

PvP
■ Player vs. player. An online game or game mode where players work against other players, either on their own or in teams.

Reboot
■ A new version of a game or game series that's designed to change the game dramatically and make it more exciting.

Remaster
■ An updated version of an old game that makes use of new graphics technology to make it look like a recent game.

Respawn
■ Coming back to life after you die in a single-player or multiplayer game, usually at a specific place (a respawn point).

Retro
■ A game or visual style that looks back to older games from the 1980s or 1990s.

Roguelike
■ A style of game where players fight through a series of randomly generated levels, killing monsters, and collecting weapons and equipment.

RPG
■ Role-playing game. A type of game where the player goes on an epic quest or adventure, fighting monsters, levelling up, and upgrading their equipment on the way.

RTS
■ Real-time strategy. A style of game where players command squads of troops, build bases to generate more troops, then use those troops to attack the enemy.

Sandbox
■ A type of game which is less about completing a set of objectives in order, and more about using objects, vehicles, and abilities in different activities and having fun.

Season pass
■ An add-on for a game that allows you to download and play through any expansions or DLC released after it launches.

Shoot 'em up
■ A style of game based on classic arcade games, where players work their way through waves of levels full of enemies, blasting away at them and avoiding their attacks.

Speedrun
■ A gaming challenge where players compete to finish a game or level in the shortest possible time.

Streaming
■ Watching a video or playing a game through a live connection to the Internet, rather than downloading it, then playing it from a console or computer.

Trolling
■ Behaving in an annoying way or saying annoying things just to provoke a reaction from other people in the game or on the Internet.

Twitch
■ A video streaming service that streams live video of players playing games.

VR
■ Virtual reality. Playing games through a head-mounted screen with motion controls so that it looks and feels more like you're actually in the game world.

XP
■ Experience points. Points scored in a game for completing objectives, beating challenges, or killing monsters, and often used to upgrade the hero, their skills, or their equipment.